EXPLORING
HOW TO
MASTER GRAMMAR

CUET, MBA, BANK(PO & CLERK)
SSC, PGT & TGT EXAMS & OTHER

Mrs. Anjali Saxena

Director, R_ambh Institute
Double M.A M.ED (ENGLISH, EDUCATION)

BLUEROSE PUBLISHERS
India | U.K.

Copyright © Anjali Saxena 2024

All rights reserved by author. No part of this publication may be reproduced, stored in a retrieval system or transmitted in any form or by any means, electronic, mechanical, photocopying, recording or otherwise, without the prior permission of the author. Although every precaution has been taken to verify the accuracy of the information contained herein, the publisher assumes no responsibility for any errors or omissions. No liability is assumed for damages that may result from the use of information contained within.

BlueRose Publishers takes no responsibility for any damages, losses, or liabilities that may arise from the use or misuse of the information, products, or services provided in this publication.

For permissions requests or inquiries regarding this publication,
please contact:

BLUEROSE PUBLISHERS
www.BlueRoseONE.com
info@bluerosepublishers.com
+91 8882 898 898
+4407342408967

ISBN: 978-93-5989-625-0

Cover design: Muskan Sachdeva

First Edition: January 2024

Dedicated
To My Parents
Mr Anil Shrivastava
&
Mrs Reetarani shrivastava
&
My husband
Mr Abhishek Saxena

GRAMMAR RULES

Subject Verb Agreement: Learners often get confused with using the appropriate form of the verb with the subject of the sentence. For example: 'I live in Thailand" and 'He lives in Thailand is the correct subject verb agreement of the verb 'to live'.

Possessive Nouns: Non-native speakers of the English are unsure about showing possession while writing or speaking in English. For example: 'The book belonging to the girl' can also be referred to as "The girl's book'.

Comparison of Adjectives: We add 'er' to compare short adjectives like pretty and thick; and we add 'more' for longer adjectives like handsome and intelligent.

Punctuation Mistakes: Punctuation errors, too, are very common, especially in the use of semicolons and commas.

Singular and Plural: Many new learners make mistakes in forming the plural form of singular nouns.

PUNCTATION RULES

Full Stop — This is the most popular punctuation mark because you simply cannot write even a single sentence without using it. So, there are two most common uses of a full stop: to indicate the end of a sentence, or to follow an abbreviation.

Comma — A comma is often used to separate ditferent ideas in a sentence. However, it has many other uses as well, and it is important to remember them as well Some of the most common comma rules follow.

Question Mark — A question mark, as its name suggests, needs to go at the end of every interogative sentence instead of a full stop.

Exclamation Mark — An exelamation mark added at the end of a sentence shows emphasis. Depending on the meaning of the sentence, it can indicate anger, happiness, excitement, or any other strong emotion

Quotation Marks — As their name suggests, quotation marks indicate direct quotations. You can also use them to show that a word or a phrase is being used ironically or for titles of articles, book chapters, episodes of a TV-show, etc

Apostrophe — An apostrophe has two very important uses. Firstly, it can be used in contractions in place of omitted letters. Secondly, it can show possession.

Hyphen — Even though it looks very similar to a dash, a hyphen has very different uses. It's most commonly used to create compound words.

Dash — There are two different dashes, the en dash and the em dash, the first being sightly shorter than the second one.

The en dash is usually used to show a connection between two things, as well as arange of numbers, years, pages, etc

Colon — A colon is a punctuation mark you will come across very often in different circumstances. It can intraduce an example, a list, an explanation, or a quotation. Or, you can also use it to emphasize a certain point.

Semicolon — A semicolon is a punctuation mark that creates a longer pause than a comma but a shorter pause than a full stop. So, it can be used to create a pause between two independent clauses that are still closely related to each other.

Parentheses — In most cases, you will see additional information in parentheses. Usually, it can be omitted without creating any confusion for the reader.

Brackets — Brackets are, in a way, similar to parentheses. However, they are mostly used in academic writing and when presenting quotes. For instance, the writer can add extra information ar fix mistakes in brackets, without changing the original quotation.

Ellipsis — An ellipsis creates an intriguing and mysterious atmosphere in the text. In addition, it can be used to show that some letters or even words are emitted.

Slash — You might need to write a fraction, a measurement, or to suggest alternatives in your text. These are just three of the instances where you will have to use a slash.

SUBJECT VERB AGREEMENT GRAMMAR RULES

- If the subject is singular, the verb must be singular. If the subject is plural, the verb must be plural. The boy is playing. / The boys are playing.

- IF two or more singular subjects are connected with "and", the verb must be plural. The dog and the cat are having lunch.

- If two or more singular subjects are Connected with "Or' or "TOr", the verb must be singular. Mollie or Linda Is organising the music.

- If the subjects include boch singular and plural nouns connected with "Or" or "nor", the verb must agree with the subject that is Closer to it. The Johnsons or Sue is coming for dinner.

- The verb must agree with the subject, not with the phrase between the subject and the verb. One of the students is missing. The students who read that story are few. The president as well as members of parliment is ready for the elections. The man in brown shoes is running.

- After the words "anybody, anyone, everybody, everyone, somebody, someone, nob ody, no one, each, each one, either, neither. you must use a singular verb. Everyone is coming to the birthday party. Somebody is knocking the front door.

- Some words end with 'S" but they are aCtually singular, so you must use a singular verb after them. (mathematics, measles, news, phonetics) The news is bad for all the family members. Phonetics is the study of sounds.

- The word money is always singular and must be followed by a singular verb. When you use currencies dollars, pounds, euros etc.", you may use a singular or plural noun depending on the meaning. If you are talking about the amount of money, you must use a singular verb. But if you are referring to the Currency itseif, you must use a plural verb. A lot of money is needed for our schol Ten pounds is good for a weekty pocket money.

- After the nouns like trousers, pants, Blasses. tweezers, shears, scissors, sunglasses you must use a plural verb. His glasses are cool, aren't they? Sallys trousers are made in Turkey. Your sunglasses really look perfect on you.

- If the subject is singular and followed by some expressions like with, including, accompanied by in addition to, as well as, we use a singular verbs. If the subiect is piural, we use a plural verb. The teacher as well as his students, is going to visit the museum. The major, accompanied by his Children, is doing some shopping. Those toys, Including the red car, are old.

- If the subiect is a collective noun, you Can use both a singula or a plural vert depending on the meaning-If you are referring a Collective nouns as a unit then use a singular verb. If you are referring the members instead, use a piural verbs. flOCK is migrating to the south. orChestra plays onty on special days. orChestra are leaving the party.

Contents

Unit 1: Vocabulary 1

Unit 2: Grammer 32

Unit 3: Reading Comprehension 107

Unit 4: Re- arranging Tumbled Up parts of a Sentence 129

ENGLISH

Unit-01　　　VOCABULARY

Means! All the words that somebody knows or that are used in a parlicalar book, subject etc.

Vocabulary - silicon cor lexicon

➢ ROOTS, PREFIX AND SUFFIX

Some different types of Roots as define

In English grammar and marphology a root is a word or word element from which others words grow, usually through the addition of prefixes and suffies.

Three types of root are there in grammar with five very forms fxit communly used words are (+) the Root the S form, Past form, ingf.

- act - to move or do (actor, acting reenact)
- arbor - tree (arbareal, arboretum arbarist)
- ego - (egofist, egocenlric, egomaniac)
- form - shape (conferm, formulati reform)
- legal - related to law (illegal, legalities, paralegal)
- meter - measure (Kilometer millimeter, pedometer)
- norm - typical (abncermal, narmality, parancermal)
- phobia - fear (arachnopobia, claustrophobia hydrophobia)

➢ Many of the words we use in our daily language come from a root word like comfartable or uncomfartable It we remove the suffix-able and prefix un-, you would be left with the root of "Comfart" To understand more lets see what is prefix arel suffix.

PREFIX

Prefix is a group of letters placed before the root of a word e.g "unhappy" the prefix "un-" combined with the root (wstem) word "happy". word "unhappy" means " not happy"

Prefix	Meaning	Examples
Circuem -	around	circumstance
de -	form	decode decrease degenerale depress
co -	with	co-worker, co-pilot Co-operation
dis	not	disagree, disallow disarray, dis loyal, disrespect
ex	cutof	exceed, exclusive exhale, xpression ex-wife, ex-faculty
mal -	bad	inalnowrishal malicious malady
macro -	large	macro-conomice macromolecule
micro -	small	microscoope microbiology microfilm microwave
pro-	before	proactive, produce, profess program
re-	again	react, reappear reform, repart revert, retrive
tarms -	acress	transatlantic transcribe transfer transform
uni -	one	unicycle, universal unilateral, unanimous

SUFFIXES

A suffix is a group of letters placed after the root of a ward. eg "flavarless" combined with the suffix - "less" means "having no flavor"

Suffix	Meaning	Examples
-able	having quality of	comfartabe partable
-a	relating to	annual comical
- ible	forming an adjective	reversible, terrible
-ily	forming an adverb	earily, happily, lazily
-ing	denoting an action material, gerrnd	acting, showing

VOCABULARY

-ish	having the quality of	childish, snobbish
-ive-	having the nature of	creative, divisive, decisive
-less	without	endless, ageless, lawless, effortless
-y	characterized by	sleazy, hasty, greasy, smelly
-er	someone who performs an action	helper, teacher, dancer
-ion	The action or process of	celebration, opinion, decion, revision
-ism	theory, act or belief	criticism, humanism, professionalism
-ity	the state or condition of	Probability, equality, abnarmatity

SYNONYMS & ANTONYMS

➢ **Synonyns** : A word or phrase that thas the same meaning as another word or phrase in the some language.

Synonyns means substitute or subremacist

Wrong	Sentence	Synoyns
Able	she is able to do her work	capable, qualified, fit, competent
Wrong	Sometimes I make a mistake and do the wrong thing	incrorrect, erroneous, inacceerale, unlawful
Cunning	She is cunning as a fox	craftty isolaing sly, wily
Resouce	I didn't need you to resue me	save release, deliverance liberation
Fantastic	It was fantastic!	Great enormous Esctravagant tremendous remarkable
Help	I couldn't help but do it	Assist guidance support aid

Say	I won't say anything to anyone	Tell, Comment, announce, declare, articulate, utter
Rich	we all dream of becoming rich	Wealthy, flash, loaded, affluent, moneyed
Naughty	Its is a naughty boy	Misbhievour disobedient lroublesome hostile venomous
Business	She runs a big business	Trade commerce, occupation, business parsuit
Neat	The movie last night was really neat,	Tidy appreciable substantial
suggest	she suggests me take the advice	propose, hint, imply, insinuate, intimale
Alike	I and my sister looked a like to be twing	some, uniform indistingwishable identical
loud	They are getting a little loud	Noisy blasting, clamorous, earsplitting
chop	chop the mushroom	cut, cleaner, axe
Trust	She trusts me	Believe, confidence,

WORDS STARTING FROM 'A'

1. **Abandon (v)**
   Syns : give up, leave, forsake
2. **Abdicate (v)**
   Syns : quit, abandon, surrender
3. **Ability (n)**
   Syns : competence, capability, talent, proficiency
4. **Abstain (v)**
   Syns : avoid, decline, refrain
5. **Abundant (adj.)**
   Syns : plentiful, full, bountiful
6. **Accuse (v)**
   Syns : blame, charge, attribute, criminate

ENGLISH

7. **Acquaint (v)**
   Syns : disclose, familiarize, inform, reveal
8. **Advantageos (adj.)**
   Syns : beneficial, profitable, gainful, convenient.
9. **Adventurous (adj.)**
   Syns : bold, daring, reckless, risky
10. **Altruistic (adj.)**
    Syns : benevolent, humane, generous, charitable
11. **Ambiguous (adj.)**
    Syns : confused, doubtful, obscure, vague
12. **Anonymous (adj.)**
    Syns : nameless, unknown, faceless, impersonal
13. **Anxiety (n)**
    Syns : desire, distress, dread, tension, worry
14. **Apathetic (adj.)**
    Syns : emotionless, impassive, indifferent, passive
15. **Aspirant (n)**
    Syns : applicant, suitor, candidate, competitor

WORDS STARTING FROM 'B'
1. **Bankrupt (adj.)**
   Syns : insolvent, ruined, spent, beggared, broke
2. **Barbarian (n)**
   Syns : boor, illiterate, philistine, savage
3. **Battalion (n)**
   Syns : army, brigade, company, regiment.
4. **Bigot (n)**
   Syns : dogmatist, racist, religionist, sexist
5. **Bureaucrat (n)**
   Syns : administrator, officer, official
6. **Brittle (adj.)**
   Syns : not tough, fragile

WORDS STARTING FROM 'C'
1. **Camouflage (n)**
   Syns : deception, disguise, blind, cloak
2. **Cemetery (n)**
   Syns : burial-ground, churchyard, graveyard
3. **Compile (v)**
   Syns : accumulate, arrange, gather, organise
4. **Cowardice (n)**
   Syns : faint-hearted, fear
5. **Credible (adj.)**
   Syns : believable, reasonable, reliable, sincere
6. **Credulous (adj.)**
   Syns : trusting, uncritical, wide-eyed

WORDS STARTING FROM 'D'
1. **Dearth (n)**
   Syns : absence, shortage, poverty, scarcity
2. **Depreciate (v)**
   Syns : decrease, reduce, minimise, devalue
3. **Dismay (v)**
   Syns : depress, disappoint, terrify, discourage, horrify
4. **Diversity (n)**
   Syns : difference, variety, range
5. **Dwarf (n)**
   Syns : elf, gnome, lilliputian, pigmy, tom thumb

WORDS STARTING FROM 'E'
1. **Emancipate (adj.)**
   Syns : deliver, discharge, free, liberate
2. **Emigration (n)**
   Syns : departure, removal, journey, migration,
3. **Exaggerate (v)**
   Syns : amplify, magnify, enlarge

WORDS STARTING FROM 'F'
1. **Fabulous (adj.)**
   Syns : amaxing, incredible, wonderful, immense
2. **Fathom (v)**
   Syns : comprehend, penetrate, work out, interpret
3. **Flammable (adj.)**
   Syns : combustible, inflammable
4. **Flourish (v)**
   Syns : bloom, develop, prosper, succeed
5. **Fragile (adj.)**
   Syns : brittle, breakable, dainty

WORDS STARTING FROM 'G'
1. **Gain (v)**
   Syns : advance, increase, progress, obtain
2. **Genial (adj.)**
   Syns : friendly, glad, happy, joyous, kind
3. **Gunman (n)**
   Syns : bandit, terrorist, killer

VOCABULARY

WORDS STARTING FROM 'H'

1. **Hazardous (adj.)**
   Syns : dangerous, risky, difficult, haphazard
2. **Hijack (v)**
   Syns : kidnap, seize, skyjack, steal,
3. **Hysteria (n)**
   Syns : madness, neurosis, panic

WORDS STARTING FROM 'I'

1. **Illuminate (v)**
   Syns : brighten, enlighten, light up
2. **Immense (adj.)**
   Syns : enormous, gigantic, great, huge, large, vast
3. **Isolated (adj.)**
   Syns : deserted, lonely, remote, solitary

WORDS STARTING FROM 'J'

1. **Juvenile (v)**
   Syns : adolescent, minor, youth

WORDS STARTING FROM 'L'

1. **Laborious (adj.)**
   Syns : industrious, laboured, uphill, tiresome
2. **Leisure (n)**
   Syns : holiday, spare time, vacation, relaxation
3. **Lethal (adj.)**
   Syns : fatal, noxious, poisonous, destructive
4. **Literal (adj.)**
   Syns : factual, exact, plain, simple, actual, strict
5. **Loathsome (adj.)**
   Syns : hateful, horrible, nasty, odious
6. **Lubricate (v)**
   Syns : grease, oil smear, wax.

WORDS STARTING FROM 'M'

1. **Malevolent (adj.)**
   Syns : hostile, vindictive, illnaured, vicious
2. **Malnutrition (n)**
   Syns : hunger, starvation
3. **Meagre (adj.)**
   Syns : inadequate, deficient, little scanty
4. **Melancholy (adj.)**
   Syns : miserable, mournful, sorrowful, unhappy
5. **Militant (adj.)**
   Syns : aggressive, fighting, vigorous
6. **Momentum (n)**
   Syns : power, strength, stimulus force, energy
7. **Mysterious (adj.)**
   Syns : curious, secret, hidden, mystical

WORDS STARTING FROM 'N'

1. **Noxious (adj.)**
   Syns : baneful, corrupting, destructive, harmful, injurious

WORDS STARTING FROM 'O'

1. **Opaque (adj.)**
   Syns : cloudy, obscure, unclear, dim
2. **Orator (n)**
   Syns : lecturer, preacher, speaker

WORDS STARTING FROM 'P'

1. **Passionate (adj.)**
   Syns : aroused, emotional, sexy, eager
2. **Pedestrian (n)**
   Syns : foot-traveller, walker
3. **Precious (adj.)**
   Syns : costly, fine, valuable, dearest
4. **Prosperous (adj.)**
   Syns : successful, rich, lucky, wealthy, fortunate
5. **Punctual (adj.)**
   Syns : early, exact, up-to-time, prompt
6. **Puzzled (adj.)**
   Syns : bewildered, doubtful, perplexed, mixed

WORDS STARTING FROM 'Q'

1. **Quaint (adj.)**
   Syns : antiquated, odd, strange
2. **Quarrelsome (adj.)**
   Syns : ill-tempered, irritable

WORDS STARTING FROM 'R'

1. **Ratify (v)**
   Syns : affirm, approve, certify, authorise
2. **Raucous (adj.)**
   Syns : harsh, hoarse, loud, noisy
3. **Rebellious (adj.)**
   Syns : disloyal, untruly, disobedient, revolutionary
4. **Referee (n)**
   Syns : arbitratr, judge, umpire
5. **Refrain (v)**
   Syns : abstain, avoid, quit
6. **Rescue (v)**
   Syns : deliver, liberate, recover, release
7. **Rogue (n)**
   Syns : cheat, deceiver, devil, villain, scoundrel

ENGLISH

WORDS STARTING FROM 'S'

1. **Scornful (adj.)**
   Syns : arrogant, defiant
2. **Seminary (n)**
   Syns : academy, college, institute, school
3. **Shriek (v)**
   Syns : howl, scream, shout
4. **Solemn (adj.)**
   Syns : caremonial, sober, momentous, ritual
5. **Spendthrift (adj.)**
   Syns : extravagant, improvident, prodigal, wasteful
6. **Stamina (n)**
   Syns : power, strength, vigour
7. **Synonymous (adj.)**
   Syns : comparable, corresponding, identical

WORDS STARTING FROM 'T'

1. **Tantamount (adj.)**
   Syns : equal, equivalent
2. **Teetotaller (n)**
   Syns : abstainer, non-drinker
3. **Tremendous (adj.)**
   Syns : excellent, exceptional, fabulous, terrific
4. **Trespasser (n)**
   Syns : criminal, infringer, intruder, offender
5. **Turbulent (adj.)**
   Syns : agitated, wild, violent, boisterous, choppy
6. **Tyrant (n)**
   Syns : autocrat, dictator, monarch, slave-driver

WORDS STARTING FROM 'U'

1. **Utterance (n)**
   Syns : announcement, statement, declaration speech

WORDS STARTING FROM 'V'

1. **Vanish (v)**
   Syns : depart, die out, disappear, disperse
2. **Veteran (n)**
   Syns : master, old hand, old timer
3. **Vigilant (adj.)**
   Syns : alert, attentive, watchful, cautious
4. **Vulgar (adj.)**
   Syns : common, boorish, native, unrefined

WORDS STARTING FROM 'W'

1. **Wrestle (v)**
   Syns : battle, combat, contend, contest

WORDS STARTING FROM 'Z'

1. **Zeal (n)**
   Syns : devotion, spirit, zest
2. **Zenith (n)**
   Syns : apex, climax, top, vertex,
3. **Zest (n)**
   Syns : appetite, charm, enjoyment, flavour

➤ **Antonyms are words that have the opposite meaning of another word**

Artificial	Natural Genevine Generous
Argue	Agree Concur Abstain Harmonize
Amaleur	Professional Expert
Adult	Child Infant Juvenile
Ancestor	Descendant Successor
Build	Destroy Demolish
Borrow	Lend Forlecit pay sharp subtle factbul
Boring	Exciting Interesting eventful livly
Ceiling	Flevor Nadir Abyss Vaulting
Calm	Excitecl Stormy Anxiety windy
Clear	Cloudy vague murky
Dictatorship	Republic Democracy Despotism Tyranny
Desperate	Itopeful Cheerful Composed meek
Domestic	Foreign undomestic untamed
Dull	Intersting Intensiby Enhance
Emigration	immigration Remaining Entrance
Expensive	Cheap moderate worthless
Eager	Apathetic Uninterested Apathetic Dispassionate
Exclude	Include Admit Approve
Exit	Entrance Arrival closure
Foreground	Background Backdrop Ground
Forbid	Allow Permit Aid
flippant	Somber Reverent courteous mannerly

VOCABULARY

gaiety	Misery Mirth Merriment
Guilty	innocent moral sinless
gentle	violent Brutal Harsh
general	Particular Restricted
Giant	Tiny miniature dwarle
Health	Disease Illness Heartiness
Nasty	Nice Agreeable Pleasant

IDIOMS AND PHRASES

Idioms : an expression whose meaning is different from the meanings of the individual words in it.

e.g : Again and Again Means many times

Phrases : A group of words that are used togther A phrase does not contain a full verb.

e.g : First of all

Starting with 'A'

	Phrases		Meaning
(1)	After all	-	Despite what has been said or escpected
(2)	At home in	-	To be strong
(3)	At the latest	-	No later than the time
(4)	At heart	-	used to say what somebody is really like
(5)	At draggers drawn with	-	To be enemies
(6)	As if	-	In a way that suggests something
(7)	At last	-	After much delay, effert
(8)	At any cost	-	As one thing of piece and not as sperate parts
(9)	A least -	-	At the lowest estimate
(10)	After a fashion	-	To Some extend, but not very well.
(11)	A lame exuse	-	weak and difficult to believe
(12)	A man of spirit	-	An enthusiastic man
(13)	A man of straw	-	A man who has not any view.
(14)	A snake in the grass	-	A secret - in the grass
(15)	An iron will	-	A firm opinion
(16)	Achilles heel	-	weak spot, valnerable point
(17)	A cake walk	-	an easy achievement
(18)	A damp squib	-	a disappointing result

Phrases Starting - 'B'

	Phrases		Meaning
(1)	Bed of roses	-	An easy or a pleasant situation
(2)	Beck and call	-	Always ready to obey somebody's under
(3)	Beat black and blue	-	To beat severely
(4)	Boso friend	-	Fast or close friend
(5)	By and by		Before long ; soon
(6)	Body and soul	-	with all your energy
(7)	By fair means of faul	-	By any means
(8)	Bird's eye view	-	A view from a high position looking down
(9)	Break the ice	-	To break the silence
(10)	Black sheep	-	Good for nothing
(11)	Bid farewell to	-	The act of saying good bye

Phrases - 'C'

	Phrases		Meaning
(1)	Come to light	-	To be revealed
(2)	Cashes in the air	-	plans or dreams that are not likely to happens
(3)	Cry in the wildervers	-	An in effective demand
(4)	Come to blow	-	to fight
(5)	Captial punishment	-	Death penalty
(6)	Chicken hearted	-	Timid
(7)	Cold blooded	-	Showing no feeling or pity for other people

Phrases -'D'

	Phrases		Meaning
(1)	Dead against	-	Just opposite
(2)	Day in, day out	-	Every day for a long period of time
(3)	Dark horse	-	One who suddenly come into light
(4)	Doubled minded	-	Confused, have different opinion
(5)	Drop in on	-	To pay an informal visit to person or a place
(6)	Drop out of	-	To no longer take part in or be part of something

ENGLISH

Phrases Starting 'F'

	Phrases		Meaning
(1)	Fair and square	-	Honestly and according to the rules
(2)	Fast living	-	Luxerious life
(3)	Fish out of water	-	To be like one out of one's element
(4)	Fool's paradise	-	Foolish ideas
(5)	Fair havel	-	legible writing
(6)	Free Lance	-	To earn money by selling your work to several different organizations
(7)	Full into a rage	-	To become angry
(8)	Full out with	-	To have an arguement with somebody
(9)	Fall behind in	-	To fail to keep level

Phrases Starting 'G'

	Phrases		Meaning
(1)	Gala day	-	A special public celebration or entertainment
(2)	gift of the gab	-	Ability or art of speaking fluently
(3)	get even with	-	to revenge
(4)	get into a soup	-	To make things difficult
(5)	get the sack	-	Dismiss from the services
(6)	go through fire and water	-	To take any risk
(7)	go to rack and rain	-	To get into a bad condition

Phrases Starting 'H'

	Phrases		Meaning
(1)	Hand up	-	Having very little money
(2)	Hard not to crack	-	A difficult problem to solve
(3)	Hand by a thread	-	A critical condition
(4)	Hand over the coals	-	To scodd, chide
(5)	Have a brush with	-	To dispute very little
(6)	Have a thing at one's	-	fingers tips - to get knowledge completely
(7)	Have clean hands	-	To get innocent
(8)	Have too many irons in the fire	-	To be engaged in too many thing

Phrases Starting 'I'

	Phrases		Meaning
(1)	Iron hand	-	with strictness
(2)	In guest of	-	In search of
(3)	In no time	-	at once
(4)	In the teeth of	-	To be against
(5)	In defence of	-	The act of protecting somebody
(6)	In view of	-	Having regard to
(7)	In respect of	-	In opionion of In the ege of
(8)	In a fix	-	In puzzling state
(9)	In a nutshell	-	In a fex words
(10)	In full swing	-	to full glory
(11)	In vogue	-	To be in fashion
(12)	Irong of fate	-	The amusing aspect of a situation that are very different from what you expect
(13)	In hot haste	-	In a hurry
(14)	In office	-	In power
(15)	In defiance of	-	Open refusal to obey

Phrases Starting 'H'

	Phrases		Meaning
(1)	Keep abreast of	-	To make sure that you know all the most recent facts about a subject
(2)	Keep body and Soul together	-	For survival
(3)	Kick a habbit	-	To stop doing something that you have done for a long time
(4)	Kill two birds with one stones	-	To serve two purposes at one time

VOCABULARY

Phrases Starting 'L'

Q.			Meaning
(1)	Look blank	-	To be amazed
(2)	learn by rote	-	To remember something without understanding
(3)	Left handed compliment	-	To complain as admiration
(4)	Langh in one's sleeves	-	To be secretly amused about someting
(5)	Lend one's ear	-	To listen
(6)	Lose one's cool	-	To lose control

Phrases Starting 'M'

	Phrases		Meaning
(1)	Make good	-	To compensate
(2)	Make up one's mind	-	To determine
(3)	Man of parts	-	A man of talent

Phrases Starting 'N'

	Phrases		Meaning
(1)	Null and void	-	Invalid
(2)	Now and again	-	Occasionally
(3)	Neck and Neck	-	side by side
(4)	Night and day	-	To be continued
(5)	Now and then	-	sometimes

Phrases Starting 'O'

	Phrases		Meaning
(1)	Offand on	-	occassionally, irregularly
(2)	on the contrary	-	The opposite of the last one
(3)	out of question	-	Not possible
(4)	once and for all	-	Now and for the last time
(5)	Once and for all	-	Now and for the last time finally or completely
(6)	out of pocket	-	without money
(7)	Open hearted man	-	A man who has an open heart
(8)	Out of one's mind	-	To be mad or crazy
(9)	On one's account	-	cause of somebody

Phrases Starting 'P'

	Phrases		Meaning
(1)	Part and parcel	-	An essential part
(2)	Pull one's weight	-	To fulfil one's duty or responsibility
(3)	To put one's head together	-	To consult with each other
(4)	Put to the sword	-	to kill

Phrases Starting 'R'

	Phrases		Meaning
(1)	A Rainy day	-	a time of difficulty or poverty
(2)	Red handed	-	To be caught doing crime

Phrases Starting 'S'

	Phrases		Meaning
(1)	Small Fry	-	Ordinary beings
(2)	sleeping partner	-	An inactive partner in business
(3)	snake in the grass	-	A hidden enemy, a deceitful person
(4)	Slip of the pen	-	A small unintiond mistake in writing
(5)	Send word	-	To send the message
(6)	Seasoned food	-	Spicy food
(7)	Set one's scheme on foot	-	To start a plan
(8)	To stand on one's own ground	-	To maintain one's own position

Phrases Starting 'T'

	Phrases		Meaning
(1)	Tooth and nail	-	With all one's resources or energy
(2)	To and fro	-	Backwords and forwards
(3)	Turn over a new leaf	-	To start a new life
(4)	Throw cold water	-	To discourage
(5)	Throw dust in one's eyes	-	To mislead
(6)	Take by storm	-	To conquer rapidly
(7)	Take the bull by the horns	-	To face a difficutlty boldly
(8)	Take to task	-	To scold

ENGLISH

Phrases Starting 'U'

	Phrases		Meaning
(1)	Up to the mark	-	up to a certain standard
(2)	An uphill task	-	An difficult work
(3)	under a cloud	-	In suspicion or disgrace
(4)	Upper hand	-	To dominant, control

Phrases Starting 'W'

	Phrases		Meaning
(1)	With respect to something	-	Concerning
(2)	A white elephant	-	A very expensive thing
(3)	Wheels within wheels	-	Complication
(4)	Will and pleasure	-	Dsire or wish
(5)	Well to do	-	rich, in good ciraumstances
(6)	walk the streets	-	prostitute
(7)	while away	-	to waste time
(8)	word in one's ears	-	to say in private
(9)	weal and woe	-	In prosperity and adversity

ONE WORD SUBSTITUTION

It refers to those tpe of question where sentence or a phrase is simple replaced by a word that describe the whole sentence.

Categories of one - word substitution

1) Generic terms
2) Government
3) Venue
4) Group
5) Death/Murder
6) Person
7) Profession
8) Sound

➢ Study - related

Study	One word	Examples
Study of stars	Astronomy	I love this book or Astronomy
Study of statistics is know as	Demography	demography of the whole town's population has been mapped
The study of ancient writing and scriptures	paleography	These three university professors have been immersed in the researcl and study of palegraphy for over a decade
The study of rocks and soil	Geoplogy	My geology home work is not going to be completed by the final submission date
The study of Human mind	Psychology	I am really interested in studying psychology and how the mind works
The study of plants	Botany	Her interests in plants motivated her pursure this course in botany
The study of language	Philology	How many languages does philology covers?

➢ Group - Collection - related

Group	One word	Examples
A group of sheep	Flock	I saw a shepherd down the hill with a flock of sheep
A family of young animals	Brood	Mr. styles like spending hours bathing the brood of horses in the stable
A number of people travelling together in a big van or jeep	Caravan	A caravan of hippies just passed by
A series of stars	Constellation	This constellation looks like a burger
A large group of people	Harde	A horde of college students were gathered arount the voting boots

VOCABULARY

Person/People - related

Person	One word	Examples
The one who loves mankind	Philanthropis	He become a renouned philanthropis after joing Buddhism
The one who looks at the brighter side of everything	optimist	Lovis has always bee the biggest optimistic person I know.
The on who looks at the negative/dark side of every thing	Pessimist	I am always on the edge of becoming a total pessimist
The one who does not believe in god	Atheist	I am neither an Atheist nor a religions person
The one who eats human flesh	Cannibal	The police caught these cannibals from the jungle.

COMMON HOMONYMS

Define: Homonyms may be words with identical pronunciations but different spellings and meanings, such as to too and two or they may be words with both identical pronunciations and identical spellings but different meanings, such as

Quail (the bird)
Quail (to cringe)

Examples are :

(1) Aunt (noun) : Aunt is the sister of one's father or mother or the wife of one's uncle

Example : My aunt won the gold medal in chess comptition

➢ Aren't - is the short form of 'are not'

   Example - we aren't going to play cricket this sunday

(2) Ate (verb) or Eight (noun)
   Ate is the past form of 'eat'
   Example : I ate a large size burger

➢ Eight - is a number
   Example - Today, I woke up at eight O' clock.

(3) Air (noun) or Heir (noun)
   Air is the invisible gaseons substand mixture mainly of oxygen and nitrogen
   Heir - A person entitled to the property or rank of another after death.

(4) Board (noun) or Bored adjective
➢ A board is a flat piece of wood.
➢ Bored means lacking interest or engagement.

(5) Dew (noun) or Due (adj,noun)
➢ Dew is tiny drops of water that form on the ground and other surfaces outside during the night when atmuspheric vapor condenses.

Eg. In the early Morning, the grass was wet with dew.

➢ Due means what is owed to one (money)

(6) Knight (noun) or Night (noun)
➢ A Knight is a man who served his souereign or lord as a mounted soldier in armor.
➢ Night is a time (Period)

(7) Leek (noun) or (leak) noun, verb)
➢ Leek is a long, white vegetable with green leaves on top that tastes and smells like an onion.

Eg. wales is famous for its rainy weather and its giant leeks

➢ leak means something is escaping (liquid or gas) from a hole or crack in a pipe or container

➢ Altar - Noun
   A holy table in a cherch or temple
   Alter - verb
   To make somebody/something different

Words Starting with 'A'

➢ Amend - verb
   To change a law, document, statement etc.
   Emend - verb
   To remove the mistaker in a piece of writing

➢ Advice - Noun
   An opinion about what somebody should do in a particular situation. Advise -verb
   To tell somebody what you think they should do in a particular situation.

ENGLISH

- Action - Noun
  a thing that somebody does
  Auction - Noun
  A public event at which things are sold to the person who offers the most money for them.
- Alien - Noun
  a creature from another world
  Align - verb
  to arrange something in the correct position
- Ailment - Noun
  an illness that is not very serious
  Element - Noun
  a simple chemical substance that consists of only one type
- Ascent - Noun
  The act of climbing ar moving up
  Assent - Noun
  official agreement to or approval of something
- Assay - Noun
  The testing of metals and chemicals for quality
  Essay - Noun
  a short piece of writing on particular subject
- Allusion - Something that is said or written that refers to or mentions another person or subject in an indirect way
  Illusion - Noun
  a false idea or belief
- Apposite - Adj.
  Very appropriate for a particular situation or in relation to something
- Opposite - Adj.
  On the other side of a particular area from somebody.
- Avacation - Noun
  A hobby or other activity that you do for interest and enjoyment
- Vocation - Noun
  A type of work or way of life that you believe is especially suitable for you.
- Abstrain - verb
  To stay away from doing something
- Refrain - Verb
  To stop your self from something
- Avert - verb
  To prevent something bad or dangerous from happening
  Revert - A return to a farmer state
- Application - Verb
  A farmal request for something such as job etc.
- Implication - Noun
  The fact of being involved or of involving somebody in something especially a crime.
- Apprehend - verb
  To understand or recognize something
- Comprehend - verb
  Understand
- Acquit - verb
  To decide and state officially in court that somebody is not guilly of a crime.
  Quit - Verb
  To leave your job, school, place etc.
- Afflict - Adj.
  Something in a unpleasant ar harmful way
- Inflict - Verb
  To make sombody suffer something unpleasant
- Alone - Adj/Adverb
  Without any other people
  Lonely - Adj
  Unhappy because you have no friends or people to talk to
- Abject - Adj.
  Without any pride or respect for yourself
  Object - Noun
  Target
- Auger - Noun
  A tool for making holes in wood
  Auger - verb
  To be a sign that something will be successful or not successful in the future.
- Accessary - Noun
  An extra piece of equipment that is useful but not essential
- Accessary - Noun
  A person who helps in any act, esp. a crime.

VOCABULARY

➤ Abjure - verb
To promise publicity that you will give up or reject a belief for a way of behaving
Adjure - verb
To ask or to order somebody to do something

➤ (a) Astronomy - Noun
The scientific study of the sun, moon, stars, planets etc.
(b) Astrology - Noun
The study of the positions of the stars and the movement of the planets in the belief that they injluence human affairs.

➤ Autumn - Noun
The season of the year between summer and winter
Autumnal - Adj
A half aged person

Words Starting With 'B'

(1) Bail - Noun
Money that some body agrees to pay if a person accused of a crime does not appear at their trial
Bale - Noun
A large amount of a light material pressed tightly together and tied up

(2) Brake - Noun
a device for slowing or stopping a vehicle
Breack - verb
To be damaged and separated into too or more parts

(3) Born - verb
To come out of your mother's body at the beginning of your life
Borne - Verb
P.P. of bear, tolerated; carried

(4) Beer - Noun
an alcholic drink made from MALT
Bear - Noun
A heavy wild animal with thick for and sharp claws
Bear - verb
To be able to accept and deal with something unpleasant

(5) Baron - Noun
A person who owns or controls a large part of a particular industry
Barren - Adj.
Injertile
Barn - Noun
A large form building for staring grain on keeping animals.

(6) Beach - Noun
Beside the sea on a lake
Bitch - Noun
A female dog

(7) Bellow - verb
A short in a long deep voice (angry)
Below - Prep.
at or to a lower level or pasition

(8) Block - Noun
a large piece of a solid material that is square in shape and usually how flat sides
Bloc - Noun
A group of Countries that work closely together because they have similar political interests.
e.g   MINC

(9) Blonde - Adj.
fair complexioned
Blond - Adj
Fair complexioned

(10) Bridal - Adj
Connected with a bride or a wedding
Bridle - Noun
A set of leather bands, which is put around a horse's head and used for controlling it
Bridle - verb
To put a bridle on a horse

(11) Boar - Noun
a wild pig
Bore - verb
To make a long deep hole with a tool or by digging

ENGLISH

(12) Breach - verb
Breack, to not keep to an agreement ar not keep a promise
Breach - Noun
A hole, a failure to do something that must to be done by low;
Breech - Noun
The part of a gun at the back where the bullets are loaded

Words Starting With 'C'

(1) (a) Cattle - Noun
Cows and bulls that are kept as form animals for their milk ar meat
(b) Kettle - Noun
a container with a lid, handle used for bailing water.

(2) Cheque - Noun
a printed farm that you write ar sign
Check - verb
To examine something to see it it is correct

(3) Canvas - Noun
A strong heavy rongh material used for making tents, sails etc.
Canvass - verb
To ask somebody to support a particular person, political party etc.

(4) Cease - Verb
To stop happing or existing
Seize - Verb
Something in your hand suddenly and using force

(5) Citi - verb
Past tense of choose
Sight - Noun
The area on distance that you can see from a particular position
Site - Noun
A place where a building town etc was located

(6) Complement - Noun
A think that adds new qualities to something in a way that improves it ar makes it attractive
Compliment - Noun
A remark that expresses praiss on admiration of somebody
Compliment - Verb
To all somebody that you like ar admire something they have done.

(7) Consistently - Adv.
Always having in the same way or having the same opionions etc.
Constantly - Adv.
All the time, repeatedly

(8) Contract - Noun
An official written agreement.
Contract - Verb
To become less or smaller

(9) Callous - adj.
Cruel unfeeling; not caring about other people feelings
Callus - Noun
An area of thick hard skin on a hand or foot, usually caused by rubbing

(10) Cannon - Noun
An old type of large heavy gun, usually on wheels that fires solid materials ar stone balls.

(11) Chair - Noun
A group of people who sing together
eg : church
Cair - Noun
Rough material made from the shells of coconuts
Card - Noun
A straight line that joins two points on a curve
Card - Noun
Strong thick string ar thin rope

(12) Corporal - Adj
A member of one of the lower ranks in the army,
Carporeal - Adj
That can be touched physical rather than spiritual for the body.

VOCABULARY

(13) Condole - verb
an expression of sympathy
Console - Verb
To give comfort or sympathy to somebody

Words Starting With 'D'

(1) Defy - Verb
To refuse to obey or show respect for somebody in authority, a law, & rule
Deify - Very
To treat or worship somebody as a god

(2) Dominant - Adj
More important, Powerful or noticeable than other things.
Domineer - verb
Try to control other people without considering their opinion or feelings
Dominate - verb
To control ar have a lot of influence over somebody/something

(3) Disposal - Noun
The sale of part of a business, property
Dispersal - Adj
The process of sending somebody/something in different directions
Dispersion - Noun
The process by which people or things are spread over a wide area
Disposition- Noun
arrangement, Temperament

(4) Distract - verb - Divert
Detract - verb - take away from
Distrust - To feel that you cannot trust ar believe somebody

Words Starting With 'E'

(1) Eligible - Adj
is able to have or do it beacuse they have the right qualification are the right age, etc
Illegible - Adj.
difficult or impossible to read

(2) Emigrant - Noun
A person who leaves their country to live in another
Immigrant - Noun
A person who has come to live permanetly in a country that is not their own

(3) Eminent - Adj
Famous and respected, especially in a particular profession
Imminent - Adj
Likely to happen very soon

(4) Elicit - Verb
To get information or a reaction from somebody aften with difficulty
Illicit - Adj - Illegal

(5) Enuelop - Verb
To wrap somebody
Enuelope - Noun
A flat paper container used for sending letters in

(6) Extinct - Adj
No longer in existence
Instinct - Noun
A natural tendency for people and animals to behave in a particular way

(7) Expert - Adj
done with having ar involving great knowledge ar skill.
Excerpt - Noun
A short piece of writing music, film etc

(8) Efficacins - Adj - Effective
Effectual - Adj.
Producing the result that was intended

(9) Exceedingly - Adv.- extremely; very much
Excessively - Adv.
Greater than what seems reasonable or appropriate

(10) Endemic - Adj
regalarly found in a particular place ar among a particular group of people and difficult to get rid of
Epidemic - Noun
A large number of cases of a particular disease happening at the same time in a particular community

ENGLISH

(11) Entomology - Noun
The scientific study of insects
Etymology- Noun
The study of the origin and history of words and their meanings

(12) Enuy- verb
To be glad that you don't have to do what some body else has to do
Enuy - Noun - Jealousy

(13) Epitaph - Noun
Words that are written or said about a dead person, especially words on a gravestone
Epithet - Noun
An offensive word or phrase that is used about a person ar group of people

(14) Excruciate - Verb
Torture; to cause mental anguish
Excuriate - verb
To irritate a persons skin so that it starts to come off
Execrate - Verb - To detest utterly

(15) Exotic - Noun
From ar in another country especially a tropical one
Erotic - Adj
Showing or involving rexual desire and pleasure

Words Starting With 'F'

(1) (a) Fair - Adj
acceptable/appropriate good, beautiful etc.
(b) Fair - Noun
An event at which at which people, business etc show and sell their goods
(c) Fare - Verb - to be successful

(2) Farther - Adv.
at or to a greater distance in space or time
Further - Adv.
In addition to what has just been said

(3) Foul - Adj - dirty and smelling bad
Fowl - Noun
A bird that is kept for its meat and eggs.

(4) Fallible - Adj.
Able to make mistakes or be wrong
Fallacious - Adj - Wrong, based on a false idea

Words Starting With 'G'

(1) Gate - Noun
a barrier like a door that is used to close an opening a fence wall outside a building
gait - Noun - a way to walking

(2) Ghastly - Adj - horrible
ghostly - Adj
looking or sounding like a ghost, full of ghosts

(3) gamble - verb
To risk money on a card game horse race etc
gambal - verb
To jump or run about in a lively way

(4) Gauge/gage - Noun
An instrument for measuring the amount or level of someting
gauze - Noun
Material made of a network of wise
Gaze - Verb - Stare
Giant - Noun
A very large strong person who is aften cruel and stupid
Gigantic - Adj
Extremely large, enormous
Gargantuar- Adj - enormous

(5) Gleam - Verb
To shine with a pale clear light
Glow - Verb
To produce a dull, steady light
glimmer- verb
to shine with a faint unsteady light

Words Starting With 'H'

(1) Heal - Verb
to become healthy again to are somebody who is ill.
Heel - Noun
The back part of the foot below the ankle

(2) Hew - Verb
To cut something large with a tool
Hue - Noun
a colour, a particular shade of a colour

VOCABULARY

(3) Handy - Adj
Skilful in using your hands or tools to make or repair things.
Handful - Adj
The amount of something that can be held in one hand

(4) Hey - interj
Used to attract somebody's altention or to express surprise, interest or anger
Hay- Noun
Grass that has been cut and dried and is used as food for animals

(5) Hoard - Noun
a connection of money food, valuable object etc
Harde - Noun
a large crowd of people.

(6) Honourable - Adj
deserving respect and admiration
Honarary- Noun
Making somebody given as an honour without the person having tro have the usual qualification

(7) Hear - Verb
to be aware of sounds with your ears
listen - Verb
to pay attention to somebody

(8) House - Noun
A building for people to live in, usually for one family
Home- Noun
The town, district that you come from or where you are living

Words Starting With 'H'
(1) (a) Idele - Adj - not working hard, lazy
(b) Ideal - Adj - perfect, most suitable
(c) idol - Noun - a statue that is warshipped as a god

(2) Ingenuous - Adj
honest, innocent and willing to trust people, noive
Ingenious - Adj
Having a lot of clever new ideas and good at inventing things

(3) Informant - Noun
A person who gives secret information about somebody
Informer - Noun
a person who gives information to the police or other anthority

(4) Imperious - Adj
expecting people to obey you and treating them as if they are not as important as you.
Imperial - Adj
Connected with an empire ; glorious, lustros.

(5) Irrelevant - Adj
not important to ar connected with a situation
Irrevenent - Adj
Not showing respect to somebody

(6) Infections - Adj
If a person or an animal is infections, they have a diseare that can be spread to others.
Contagious - Adj
a contagious disease spreads by people touching each other

(7) Interment - Noun
The act of burying a dead person, burial
Internment - Noun
Confinement within prescribed limits

Words Starting With 'J'
(1) Judicial - Adj
Connected with a court, a judge ar legal judgement
Judicious - Adj
Careful and sensible showing good judgement

(2) Test - Noun
Something said ar done to amuse people, joke
Zest - Noun
enjoyment and enthesiasn appetite

(3) Jocular - Adj - humorons
Jocund - Adj - Cheerful
Jovial - Adj - Very cheerful and friendly

(4) Juvenile - Adj
Connected with young people who are not yet adults
Jejune - Adj - too simple, naive

ENGLISH

Words Starting With 'K'

(1) Knotty - Adj
Complicated ar diffciult to solve, thorny
Naughty - Adj
behaving badly

(2) Knot - Noun
A join made by tying together two pieces or ends of string, rope etc
Naught - Noun
Used in particular phrases to mean 'nothing'

Words Starting With 'L'

(1) Loth - Adj - Not willing to do something
Loathe - verb - to dislike somebody

(2) Licence - Noun
an official document that shows permission has been given to do, own or use something
Licence - verb to give somebody official permission to do, own

(3) Latitudes - Noun
The distance of a place east or west of the greenwich meridian, measused, in degrees

(4) Licentions - Adj
Behaving in a way that is considered sexually immoral
Lascivious - Adj - Feeling ar showing strong sexual desire
Lecherons - Adj - having too much interest in sexual pleasure.

(5) Linage - Noun
related to the number of lives
Lineage - Noun
The series of families that somebody comes from originally

(6) Liquor - Noun
a strong sweet alcoholic drink.

Words Starting With 'M'

(1) Moral - Noun
Standards ar principles of good behaviour, especially in matters of sexual relationship.
Morale - Noun
The amount of confidence and enthusiasm etc that a person ar a group has a particular time.

(2) Magnet - Noun
a piece of iron that altracts objects made of iron towards it
Magnate - Noun
a person who is rich, powerful and successful especially in business

(3) Marital - Adj
Connected with marriage or with the relationship between a husband and wife
Marshal - Noun
An officer of the highest rank in the britist Army or Air force

(4) Momentary - Adj - Lasting for a very short time, briefly
Momentons - Adj - Very important or serious

(5) Meter - Noun
A device that measures and records the amount of electricity, gas, water, etc.
Metre - Noun
A unit for measuring length e.g a hunderd centimetres.

(6) Mayor - Noun - The head of a town (government)
Mare - Noun - a female horse or donkey

(7) Meretricious - Adj
Seeming attractive, but in fact having no real value
Meritarious - Adj
deserving praise, praise warthy

(8) Misogynist - Noun - A man who hater woman
Misogamist - Noun - Later of marriage

(9) Mitigate - Verb - To make something less harmful, serious etc.
Militate - verb - To prevent something

(10) Monogram - Noun
Two or more letters, usually the first letters of somebody's names
Monograph - Noun
a detailed written study of a single subject, usually in the form of short book

VOCABULARY

Words Starting With 'N'

(1) Naval - Adj
Connected with the navy of a country
Navel - Noun
The shall hollow part ar lump in the middle of the stomach where the umbilical cord was cut at birth

(2) Naught - Noun - nothing, a cipher, zero, destruction
Nought - Noun - nothing, rain, zero

(3) Nefarious - Adj - Criminal, immoral
Felonious - Adj - relating to or involved in crime

Words Starting With 'O'

(1) Ordinance - Noun
and order or a rule made by a government.

(2) ordnance - Noun
Large guns on wheels

(3) Oar - Noun
A long pole with a flat blade at one end that is used for rowing a boat

(4) One - Noun
Rock, earth, etc from which metal can be obtainel

(5) Odious - Adj
extremely unpleasant heerrible

(6) Order - Noun
Something that somebody is told to do by somebody in anthority.

(7) Obscure - Adj - difficult to undrstant not well known

(8) Obstacle - Noun
a situation an event etc that makes it difficult for you do or achieve something
Obstinate - Adj
refusing to change your opinions, way of behaving etc.

(9) Odium - Noun
A feeling of hatrel that a lot of people have towards somebody because of something they have done.

(10) Odour - Noun - A smell, especially one that is unpleasant

(11) Oppresion - Noun
Act of oppressing ar state of being oppressed, mental distress,
Repression - Noun
The act of using force to control a group of people and restrict their freedom

(12) Outrageous - Adj
Very shocking and unacceptable, scandalons
Outre - Adj
Very unuabual and slightly shocking

Words Starting With 'P'

(1) Pole - Noun
A long thin straight piece of wood or metal especially one with the end placed in the ground
Poll - Noun
toch the process of voting at an election

(2) Persecute - verb
to treat somebody in a cruel and unfair way
Prosecute - verb
to officially charge somebody with a crime in court.

(3) Prescribe - Verb
to tell somebody to take a particular medicine or have a particular treatment
Proscribe - Verb
to say officially that something is banned.

(4) Plane - Noun - A flying vehicle with wings
Plain - Adj - not decorated or complicated
Plan - Noun - something that you intend to do or achieve

(5) Physic - Noun - Any medicinine, a drug or medicament
Physique - Noun - The size and shape of a person's body
Physics - Noun
The scientific study of matter and energy and the relationship bet them

ENGLISH

(6) **Pair** - Noun
Two things of the same type, especially when they are used or more together
Pare - verb -
to cut away the edge to something, especially your nails.

(7) **Peal** - Noun
a loud sound or serious of sounds
Peel (off) - verb
to take the skin off fruit vegetable etc
Peel - verb
To take the skin off fruit vegetable etc.

(8) **Pedal** - Noun
a flat bar on a machine such as a bicycle, car etc.
Paddle - Noun
a short pole with a flat wide part at one or both ends.

(9) **Pitiable** - Adj - deserving pity ar causing you to feel pity
Piteous - Adj - Pathetic
Pitiful - Adj - Not deserving respect

(10) **Permeate** - Verb - To spread to every part of an Object ar a place
Permete - Verb - to alter the order of

(11) **Palate** - Verb - to examine part of the body by touching
Palpitate - Verb
To beat rapidly and/ar in an Irregular way especially because of fear ar exitment

(12) **Parlour** - Adj - Very bad, dangerous or uncertain, perilous
Perilous - Adj - Very dangerour

(13) **Pendant** - Noun
A piece of jewellery that you wear around your neck on a chain.
Pendent - Adj
Hanging, over hanging

(14) **Picturesque** - Adj - of a place (old) building
Picaresque - Adj
Connected with literature that describes the adventures of a person who is sometimes dishonest but easy to like

(15) **Predominate** - Verb
to be greater in amount ar number than something
Preponderate - Verb
To out weigh; to be hecwier than, number etc

(16) **Prolific** - Adj.
(of plants, animals etc) Producing lot of fruit
Prolix - Adj
(of writing, a speech, etc) using too many words

Starting With 'Q'

(1) **Query** - Noun
A question, especially one asking for information ar expressing a doubl about something
Quarry - Noun
A place where large amounts of stone etc are dug out of the ground.

(2) **Quarre/some** - Adj
liking to argue with people
Querulous - Adj - complaining ; peevish

(3) **Quota** - Noun
The limited number ar amount of people ar things
Quorum - Noun
The smallest number ar amount of people who must be at a meeting before.

Words Starting With 'R'

(1) **Reign** - Verb - to rule as king, queen emper or etc.
Rein - Noun
A long narrow leather band that is fastened around a here s neck and is held by the ride in order to control the horse

(2) **Root** - Noun
The part of plant that grows under the ground and abgorbs water and minerals that it sends to the rest of the plant.
Ronte - Noun
A way that you follow to get from one place to another

VOCABULARY

(3) Right - Noun
A moral or legal claim to have ar get something ar to behave in a particular way
Right - Adj - Morally good ar acceptable

(4) Refuse - Verb - to say that you will not give somebody
Refuge - Noun - shelter ar protection from danger, trouble etc

(5) Raise - verb - to lift or move something to a higher level
Raze - verb - to completely destroy a building town etc
Rays - Noun - Narrow lines of light heat ar other evergy
Rise - verb - to get up from lying
Razz - Verb
to tease somebody by saying ar doing things to make people laugh at them

(6) Revel - Verb
to spend time enjoying yourself in a noisy, enthusiastic way, make erry.
Reveal - verb
to make something known to somebody ; disolose.

(7) Ravage - Verb
do damage something badly ; devastate
Ravish - verb
(of a man) to force a woamn to have sex, Rape, to give somebody great pleasure

(8) Rebut - verb
to say or prove that a statement or criticism is false ; Refute
Rebuff - verb
an unkind refusal of a friendly offer, request or suggestion, Rejection.

(9) Reliable - Adj.
that can be trusted to do something well, that you can rely on, dependable
Reliant - Adj
Needing somebody/something
inordertosurvive, besuccessful, etc. dependent

(10) Reluetant - Adj
hesitating before doing something because you don't want to do it or because you are not sure that it is the right thing to do.
Reticent - Adj - disposed to be silent, Reserved.

(11) Repel - Verb
to drive, push or keep something away, to make somebody feel horror or disgust, disgust repulse, to successfully fight somebody who is attacking you, your country etc and drive them away.
Repulse - Verb
to make somebody feel disgust or strong dislike, repel, to refuse to accept somebody's help, attempts to be friendly, etc, reject.

(12) Resin - Noun
A sticky substance that is produced by some trees & is used in making varnigh, medicine etc.
Rosin - Noun
A substance that is used on the bow of a musical instrument such as violin so that it moves across the strings more easily.

(13) Reverent - Adj - Showing great respect & admiration, respectful
Reverend - Adj
The title of a member of the clergy that is also sometimes used to talk to or about one.

(14) Risky - Adj
Involving the possibility of something bad happening, dangerous.
Risque - Adj
Daringly close to indirect or impropriety.

(15) Rouse - Verb
To wake somebody up , especially when they are sleeping deeply, to make somebody engry, excited or full of emotion.
Arouse - Verb
to make somebody feel sexually excited, excite, to wake somebody from sleep.

ENGLISH

(16) Royal - Adj
Connected with or belonging to the king or queen of a country,
Regal - Adj
A typical of a king or queen & therefore impressive, royal fit for a monarch, stately, splendid.

Words Starting With 'S'

(1) Story - Noun
A description of events & people that the writer or speaker has invented in order to entertain people.
Storey - Noun - A level of a building

(2) Sensible - Adj
(of people & their behaviour) able to make good judgements based on reason & experience rathen than emotion, practical.
Senstitive - Adj
Aware of & able to understand other people & their feeling.

(3) Spectacle - Noun
A Singh or view that is very impressive to look at.
Spectacles - Noun - Glasses

(4) Seize - Verb
to take somebody/something in your hand suddenly & using force, grab
Siege - Noun
A military operation in which an army tries to capture a town by surrounding it & stopping the supply of food, etc to the people inside.
Cease - Verb
to stop happening or existing, to stop something from happening or existing.

(5) Stimulus - Noun
Something that produces a reaction in a human, an animal or a plant.
Stimulant - Noun
A drug or substance that makes you feel more awake & gives you more energy.

(6) Suit - Noun
A set of clothes made of the same cloth, including a jacket & trousr / pants or a skirt.
Suit - verb
To be convenient or useful for somebody, to be right or good for somebody/ something
Suite- Noun
A set of rooms, espicially in a hotel
Soot - Noun
black powder that is produced when wood, coal etc is burnt.

(7) Stable - Noun - A building in which horses are kept.
Staple - Noun
A small piece of wire that is used in a device called a stapler & is pushed through pieces of paper & bent over at the ends in order to fasten the pieces of paper together.

(8) Stress - Noun
Mental pressure, physical pressure, Emphasis.
Strain - Noun
Worry, Anxiety, physical pressure.

(9) Strict - Adj
that must be obeyed exactly, obeying the rules of a particular, religion, belief etc exactly, very exact & clearly defind.
Stringent - Adj
(of a law, rule, regulation) very strict & that must be obeyed, (of financial condition) difficult & very strictly controlled because there is not much money.

(10) Supersede - Verb
to take the place of something/somebody that is considered to be old fashioned or no longer the best available.
Surpass - verb
To do or be better than somebody/something, to be high quality or degree to be excelled, to be exceptional to be unparalleled.

VOCABULARY

(11) Suspense - Noun
uncertainty ; anxiety ; undecided or doubtful condition as of affairs
Subspension - Noun
A state of uncertainty ; anxiety ; a temporary abrogation or deferment; The act of officially removing somebody from their job, school, team etc for a period of time, usually as a punishment ; the act of delaying something for a period of time, until a decision has been taken.

(12) Sympathy - Noun
the feeling of being sorry for somebody ; showing that you understand and care about somebody's problems
Empathy - Noun
theability to understand another person's feelings, experience etc

Words Starting With 'T'

(1) Tale - Noun
A tale created using the imagination, especially one the is full of action and adventure
Tail - Noun
the part that sticks out and can be moved at the back of the body of a bird, an animal or a fish

(2) Throne - Noun
A special chair used by a king or queen to sit on at ceremonies
Thrown - Verb
sent something from your hand through the air by moving your hand or arm quickly

(3) Teem - Verb
(of rain) to fall heavily ; pour
Teem with something - Phrasal Verb
to be full of people, animals etc moving around

(4) Temper - Noun
A short period of feeling very angry
Tamper - Verb
to make changes to something without permission especially in order to damage it
Tamper with something - phrasal - Interfere with

(5) Transient - Adj.
continuing for only a short time ; fleeting ; temporary
Transitory - Adj.
continuing for only a short time ; fleeting Temporary

(6) Tortuous - Adj.
not simple and direct; long, complicated and difficult to understand; convoluted; full of bends, winding
Torturous - Adj.
having mental or physical suffering; Tormented

(7) Tense - Adj.
(of a person) nervous or worried and unable to relax
Terse - Adj.
using few words and often not seeming polite or friendly

(8) Terminal - Noun/ Adj.
A place, building or set of buildings where journeys by train, bus or boat begin or end ; at the end of something ; that cannot be curved and will lead to death, often slowly
Terminus - Noun
the last station at the end of a railway/rail road line or the last stop on a bus route

(9) Testament - Noun
a thing that shows that something else exits or it true; Testimony; will
Testimony - Noun
a thing that shows that something else exists or is tue ; Testament

(10) Traverse - Noun
an act of moving side ways or walking across a steep slope, not climbing up or down it, A place where this is possible or necessary
Transverse - Adj.
Placed across something ; Diagonal

ENGLISH

(11) Troop - Noun
soldiers, especially in a large groups; one groups of soldiers, especially in tanks or on horses
Troupe - Noun
A group of actors, singers etc. who work together

(12) Tumult - Noun
A confused situation in which there is usuall a lot of noise and excitement, often involving large numbers of people.
Turmoil - Noun
A state of great anxiety and confusion ; confusion

(13) Turpid - Adj. - mean ; wicked
Torpid - Adj.
not active ; with no energy and enthusiasm ; lethargic

Words Starting With 'U'

(1) Umpire - Noun
A person whose job is to watch a game and make sure that rules are not broken
Empire - Noun
A group of countries or states that are controlled by one ruler or government

(2) Unwanted - Adj. - that you donot want
Unwonted - Adj. - not usual or expected

Words Starting With 'V'

(1) Venal - Adj.
Prepared to do dishonest or immoral things in return for money ; corrupt
Venial - Adj.
(of a sin or mistake) not very serious and there fore able to be forgiven

(2) Vacation - Noun
one of the perikods of time when universities or courts of law are closed; Holiday
Vocation - Noun
A belief that a particular type of work or way of life is especially suitable for you ; calling
Avocation - Adj.
A hobby or other activity that you do for interest and enjoyment

(3) Venture - Noun
A business project or activity, especially one that involves taking risks ; undertaking
Adventure - Noun
An unusual, exciting or dangerous experience, journey or series of events

(4) Violent - Adj.
involving or caused by physical force that is intended to hurt or kill somebody ; very strong and sudden ; intense, severe
Virulent - Adj.
extremely dangerous or harmful and quick to have an effect; showing strong negative and bitter feelings
Vehement - Adj.
showing very strong feeling, especially enger, forceful

Words Starting With 'W'

(1) Waive - Verb
to choose not to demand something in a particular case even though you have a legal oir official right to do so ; Forgo ; not insist on
Wave - Verb
to move your hand or arm from side to side in the air in order to attract attention ; to show where something is, show somebody where to go etc. by moving your hand in a particular direction

(2) Wreath - Noun
a circle of flowers or leaves worn on the head, and used in the past as a sign of honour
Wreathe - Verb
to surround or cover something, to move slowly and lightly, especially in circles ; weave

(3) Wear - Verb
to have something on your body as a piece of clothing, a decoration etc
Ware - Noun
objects made of the material or in the way or place mentioned
Were - Verb
strong form of 'be' ; Auxiliary verb used in past tense

VOCABULARY

(4) Wet - Adj.
covered with or containing liquid especially water
Whet - Verb
to sharpen by grinding or friction ; to increase your desire for or interest in something

(5) Wriggle - Verb
to wist and turn your body or part of it with quick short movements ; wiggle ; squirm
Wiggle - Verb
to move from side to side or up and down in short quick movements ; Wriggle

(6) Wink - Verb
to close one eye and open it again quickly, especially as a private signal to somebody or to show something is a joke ; to shine with a unsteady light ; to flash on and off, blink
Blink - Verb
to shine with an unsteady light ; to flash on and off

Words Starting With 'Y'

(1) Yoke - Noun
A long piece of wood that is fastened across the necks of two animals, especially oxen, so that they can pull heavy loads
Yolk - Noun
the round yellow part in the middle of an egg

PRACTICE SET

Q.1 Fill in the blanks with suitable words given in the brackets:

1. He can not .... my offer. **(accept/except)**
2. All .... Aditya were present in the class. **(except/eccept)**
3. You cannot............ to my request. **(accept/exceed)**
4. Does your expenditure .... your income? **(exceed/eccede)**
5. I have no .... to the Chief Minister. **(access/excess)**
6. Your income should not be in ..... to your income. **(excess/access)**
7. I gave him a piece of .... **(advice/advise)**
8. I .... him to give up smoking **(advised/adviced)**
9. We should ..... ourselves to the changing circumstances. **(adapt/adopt/adept)**
10. The method which you have .... is wrong. **(adopted / adapted)**
11. Hema is .... in dancing. **(adept / adopt / adapt)**
12. The driver met with a serious .... **(accident /incident)**
13. Mr. Thakur related an interesting .... in his life. **(incident / accident)**
14. The people of ...... countries are very hard working. **(occident/accident)**
15. True love does not .... with the passing of time. **(alter/altar)**
16. Gandhijee died at the .... of his mother land. **(alter/altar)**
17. We are .... to drinking, it ruins health. **(averse / adverse)**
18. Due to .... circumstances he cannot pay his college dues. **(adverse/averse)**
19. Overwork .... my health. **(affected / effected)**
20. My advice had no .... on him. **(effect/effect)**
21. Our teacher explained the .... in the drama. **(allusions/illusions)**
22. She thought that she had seen a ghost, but it was only an .... **(illusion / allusion)**
23. Gardening is my .... **(avocation/vocation)**

ENGLISH

24. Teaching is his .... (vocation/avocation)
25. The police ...... the pickpocket. (apprehended/comprehended)
26. He cannot .... this scheme. (comprehend/apprehend)
27. He .... the murder of his brother by getting the murderer hanged. (avenged / revenged)
28. He .... himself on his enemy. (revenged / avenged)
29. The communal ...... swed the seed of Pakistan. (award / reward)
30. I will give you a .... if you top the list in the university. (reward/award)
31. The soldiers made another .... to climb the hill, but failed. (assay / essay)
32. His .... was adjudged to be the best one. (essay / assay)
33. He is an ...... man. (artful /arficial)
34. He does not believe in .... acting. (artificial / artful)
35. Mahatma Gandhi was .... in 1948. (assassinated / killed)
36. The hunter .... the lion. (killed/assassinated)
37. May I know your date of ....? (birth / berth)
38. Please reserve the lower .... in the train. (berth/birth)
39. Do not walk .... footed. (bare / bear)
40. I cannot .... this insult. (bear / bare)
41. The accused has been released on .... (bail / bale)
42. The .... of cotton are still lying here. (bales / bails)
43. One can not control a horse without a .... (bridle/bridal)
44. She looks graceful in her .... dress. (bridal / bridle)
45. I was .... in 1970. (born / borne)
46. He has .... many sufferings. (borne/born)
47. The daughter is sitting .... her mother. (baside/ besides)
48. .... this turban, he has two more. (besides/beside)
49. Akbar was a .... ruler. (benevolent, beneficial)
50. Exercise is .... for health. (beneficial / beneficiary)

ANSWERS WITH EXPLANATION

Q.1 Ans.
1. accept
2. except
3. exceed
4. exceed
5. access
6. excess
7. advice
8. advised
9. adapt
10. adopted
11. adept
12. accident
13. incident
14. occident
15. alter
16. altar
17. averse
18. adverse
19. affected
20. effect
21. allusions
22. illusion
23. avocation
24. vocation
25. apprehended
26. comprehend
27. avenged
28. revenged
29. award
30. reward
31. assay
32. essay
33. artful
34. artifical
35. assassinated
36. killed
37. birth
38. berth
39. bare
40. bear
41. bail
42. bales
43. bridle
44. bridal
45. born
46. borne
47. beside
48. besides
49. benevolent
50. Beneficial

VOCABULARY

PRACTICE SET

Q.1 Choose the option that describes the meaning of each of the following idioms and phrases:

1. To catch a Tartar :
   (a) To live carefully and cautiously
   (b) To catch a dangerous person
   (c) To trap a wanted criminal with great difficulty
   (d) To deal with a person who is more than one's match

2. End in smoke :
   (a) produce good results
   (b) bear no fruit
   (c) benefit the poor and downtrodden
   (d) motivate to produce

3. In the blues :
   (a) being colourful
   (b) behave like a fool
   (c) melancholic and low spirited
   (d) having many blue things

4. To turn over a new leaf :
   (a) to divert from the path
   (b) to disclose a secret
   (c) to destroy a leaf
   (d) to commence a new course of life

5. To smeel a rat :
   (a) to be in a bad mood
   (b) To suspect foul dealings
   (c) bad smell
   (d) sings of plague epidemic

6. A man of straw :
   (a) a man of no substance
   (b) an unreasonable person
   (c) a worthy fellow
   (d) a very active person

7. To fall flat :
   (a) to retreat
   (b) to meet accidentally
   (c) to be met with a cold reception
   (d) to quarrel

8. To cast pearls before swine :
   (a) to offer a person, a thing wich he can't appreciate
   (b) to waste money over trifles
   (c) to spend a lot of money on the upkeep of domestic dogs
   (d) to spend recklessly

9. A wet blanket :
   (a) a man who is always drunk
   (b) a wife who is cold to her husband
   (c) to wear black and white clothes
   (d) none of these

10. To carry the coal to New castle:
    (a) to do the mental jobs
    (b) to finish a difficult job
    (c) to do an unnecessary job
    (d) to work very hard

11. To lose one's bearings :
    (a) to lose one's strength
    (b) to become sick and tired
    (c) to be uncertain of one's position
    (d) to become hopeless

12. To keep one's temper :
    (a) to be in a good mood
    (b) to become angry
    (c) to preserve one's energy
    (d) to be a loof from

13. To draw the line :
    (a) to decide one's occupation
    (b) to prepare for a battle
    (c) to set limits
    (d) to with draw from activity

14. Right hand man :
    (a) a foolish person
    (b) most efficient assistant
    (c) an honest person
    (d) one who cannot use his hand

15. A pipe dream :
    (a) a bad dream
    (b) a pleasant dream
    (c) an impracticable plan
    (d) a foolish idea

ENGLISH

16. The green eyed monster:
    (a) the creature of the sea
    (b) animal with green eyes
    (c) personal jealousy
    (d) to get into trouble

17. Dog in the manger :
    (a) a person who has no home
    (b) a person who is not liked by others
    (c) a person who prevents others from enjoying something useless to him
    (d) a person who puts himself in difficulty on account of other people

18. Will-o' the wisp :
    (a) to act ina childish way
    (b) to act in a foolish way
    (c) anything which eludes or deceives
    (d) to have desires unbacked b efforts

19. To bite the dust :
    (a) to be defeated in a battle
    (b) to learn a lesson
    (c) to be ashamed of
    (d) to work very hard

20. To get into hot waters:
    (a) to suffer a financial loss
    (b) to be impatient
    (c) to get into trouble
    (d) to be in a confused state of mind

21. To cool one's heels :
    (a) to be kept waiting for sometime
    (b) to rest for sometime
    (c) to reamin in a comfortable position
    (d) to give no importance to someone

22. The pros and cons :
    (a) good and evil
    (b) former and latter
    (c) foul and fair
    (d) for and against a thing

23. Above board :
    (a) friendly
    (b) able to face difficulties
    (c) honestly
    (d) hard working

24. Adhoc :
    (a) for the special purpose
    (b) arranged systematically
    (c) arranged in order
    (d) none of these

25. Ante meridian :
    (a) an old mother
    (b) a greater mother
    (c) between midnight and noon
    (d) none of these

Q.2 What do the following idioms and phrases mean?
1. At sixes and sevens.
2. A queer fish.
3. A fish out water
4. At a pinch.
5. To read between the lines
6. A hue and cry
7. To hang fire
8. To bury the hatchet
9. To put one's foot down
10. To live in an Ivory tower

Q.3 Choose the suitable option that describes the meaning of the words or phrases printed in italics in each of the following sentences :

1. Please *look into* the matter personally as it is very important
   (a) see secretly   (b) examine
   (c) take care of   (d) overlook

2. Everybody is worried about his bread and butter these days
   (a) promotional avenues
   (b) comfortable living
   (c) money making
   (d) means of livelihood

3. The old man is hard of hearing :
   (a) felt bad hearing the news
   (b) somewhat deaf
   (c) does not pay
   (d) unmindful

VOCABULARY

4. Napolean won his laurels in the Battle of Waterloo :
   (a) acquired distinction
   (b) defeated the enemies
   (c) adopted aggressive attitude
   (d) surrendered to his opponents

5. Sumit had to look high and low before he could find his scooter key :
   (a) nowhere   (b) always
   (c) everywhere   (d) somewhere

6. My neighbour had to pay through his nose for a brand new car. :
   (a) pay huge loans
   (b) pay a reasonable price
   (c) pay an extremely high price
   (d) make a quick buck

7. The expression to be born with a silver spoon in one's mouth means :
   (a) to be born in a rich family
   (b) to be born as the first child
   (c) to be born in a jeweller's family
   (d) to be spoon fed, not breast fed

8. In life we have to take the rough with the smooth :
   (a) be tough in order to be successful
   (b) say pleasant words to make things smooth
   (c) accept unpleasant as well as pleasant things
   (d) make unpleasant things better

9. She was in a *brown study* and did not notice my entrance
   (a) reverie   (b) fear
   (c) dream   (d) sleep

10. They sold his house because it was a real white elephat :
    (a) an expensive one   (b) a big one
    (c) a useless one   (d) a rare thing

11. His rough behaviour would make him bite the dust :
    (a) make a plan   (b) eat the dust
    (c) get humiliated   (d) get killed

12. In the fight he was beaten nech and crop :
    (a) softly   (b) profoundly
    (c) completely   (d) swiftly

13. If one aids and abets a criminal, he is also considered guilty of crime :
    (a) suspicious   (b) daring
    (c) culpable   (d) ruthless

14. During the last moments of his life, the criminal made a clean breast of everything he had done:
    (a) showed his breast
    (b) fought like a hero
    (c) confessed without reserve
    (d) faced bravely

15. I saw him make a dry face :
    (a) abuse
    (b) feel sick
    (c) cry with pain
    (d) show disappointment

Q.4 **Fill in the blanks choosing the suitable option given below each sentence:**

11. The teacher gives many examples to .... the idea contained in the poem.
    (a) bring about   (b) bring in
    (c) bring forth   (d) bring out

12. Ram agreed to ...... my orders.
    (a) carry away   (b) carry on
    (c) carry out   (d) carry off

13. He generally .... at an odd hour.
    (a) turns over   (b) turns on
    (c) turns up   (d) turns off

14. On account of overwork, he is ....
    (a) run down   (b) runs down
    (c) ran out   (d) run up

15. Rita always sets her alarm so that she can ..... at 8 a.m.
    (a) think over   (b) write down
    (c) think through (d) wake up

ENGLISH

16. The old man .... without any trouble last night.
    (a) passed away   (b) passed for
    (c) passed by   (d) passed out

17. The doctor advised me to ...... drinking.
    (a) give out   (b) give up
    (c) give back   (d) give over

18. I have .... the business to my eldest son.
    (a) handed out   (b) handed over
    (c) handed round   (d) handed back

19. The sick man .... last night.
    (a) passed away   (b) passed by
    (c) passed down   (d) passed for

20. You are unable to .... the meaning of this passage.
    (a) make off   (b) make out
    (c) make over   (d) make up

Q.5 Choose the suitable option that describes the meaning of the words or phrases printed in italics in each of the following sentences :

16. He frequently goes back on his words.
    (a) repeat his words
    (b) confuses others
    (c) stumbles
    (d) breaks his promises

17. I cannot make out what yu say.
    (a) rely upon   (b) believe
    (c) understand   (d) solve

18. The party high command wanted to stave off an open battle.
    (a) postpone
    (b) wait and see
    (c) allow it to take its own course
    (d) prevent

19. No one but his conscience advised him to come back to earth.
    (a) return home   (b) return to earth
    (c) return to reality (d) be honest

20. Ramesh takes after his father.
    (a) follows   (b) imitates
    (c) obeys   (d) resembles

21. The country's economy is beginning to look up now.
    (a) remain static   (b) improve
    (c) look clear   (d) go down

22. I cannot put up with that nasty fellow.
    (a) appreciate   (b) endure
    (c) control (d) forgive

23. To look quickly through a book is an important study skill.
    (a) to skim (b) to summarize
    (c) to outline   (d) to paraphrase.

24. As she was turning out some papers she came across the letter she had been loking for.
    (a) saw from a distance
    (b) found unexpectedly
    (c) touched
    (d) read quickly

25. She tries very hard to keep up with her rich neighbours.
    (a) to imitate   (b) to keep touch
    (c) to avoid   (d) to be on par

Q.6 Substitute the italicised idiomatic expression with an appropriate word/phrase without changing the meaning of the sentence:

1. He backed up his friends claim.
2. The present disturbances will soon blow over.
3. I have hit upon a good plan to get rid of him.
4. The matter has been cleared off and will soon be settled.
5. I must think over the matter before taking a final decision.
6. He broke down in the middle of his speech.
7. His folly has brought about his rain.
8. He has made up his mind to be a doctor.
9. She did not put back home last night.
10. He has entered upon a good career.

VOCABULARY

ANSWERS WITH EXPLANATION

Q.1 Ans.
1. (d) 2. (a) 3. (c) 4. (d) 5. (a)
6. (b) 7. (c) 8. (a) 9. (d) 10. (d)
11. (c) 12. (e) 13. (c) 14. (a) 15. (c)
16. (c) 17. (c) 18. (c) 19. (a) 20. (c)
21. (a) 22. (d) 23. (c) 24. (a) 25. (c)

Q.2 Ans.
1. in disorder
2. A strange fellow
3. In an uncomfortable position
4. If absolutely necessary, if circumstances make it essential
5. To understand the hidden meaning
6. A great stir
7. Linger on
8. For get a quarrel
9. To reject with determination
10. To be unaware of the realities

Q.3 Ans.
1. (b) 2. (d) 3. (b) 4. (a) 5. (c)
6. (c) 7. (a) 8. (c) 9. (a) 10. (c)
11. (c) 12. (c) 13. (c) 14. (c) 15. (d)

Q.4 Ans.
1. (a) 2. (c) 3. (c) 4. (a) 5. (d)
6. (a) 7. (b) 8. (b) 9. (a) 10. (b)

Q.5 Ans.
1. (d) 2. (c) 3. (d) 4. (c) 5. (d)
6. (b) 7. (b) 8. (a) 9. (b) 10. (a)

Note : Skim (V) = to read something quickly in order to find a particular point or the main points.

Q.6 Ans.
1. backed up : supported
2. blow over : pass by, be forgotten
3. hit upon : fount by chance or unexpectedly
4. cleared off : got rid of, made an end of.
5. Think over : consider further.
6. broke down : collapsed.
7. brought about : caused to happen.
8. made up : came to a decision.
9. put back : return
10. entered upon : made a start on.

ENGLISH

ANSWERS WITH EXPLANATION

Q. 1 Ans.

#		#		#	
1.	accept	17.	averse	34.	artifical
2.	except	18.	adverse	35.	assassinated
3.	exceed	19.	affected	36.	killed
4.	exceed	20.	effect	37.	birth
5.	access	21.	allusions	38.	berth
6.	excess	22.	illusion	39.	bare
7.	advice	23.	avocation	40.	bear
8.	advised	24.	vocation	41.	bail
9.	adapt	25.	apprehended	42.	bales
10.	adopted	26.	comprehend	43.	bridle
11.	adept	27.	avenged	44.	bridal
12.	accident	28.	revenged	45.	born
13.	incident	29.	award	46.	borne
14.	occident	30.	reward	47.	beside
15.	alter	31.	assay	48.	besides
16.	altar	32.	essay	49.	benevolent
		33.	artful	50.	beneficial

Unit-02 GRAMMAR

ARTICLES

A, An and The are known as Articles generally there are used before nouns. These are Adjective In modern English grammar. These are also known as Determiners.

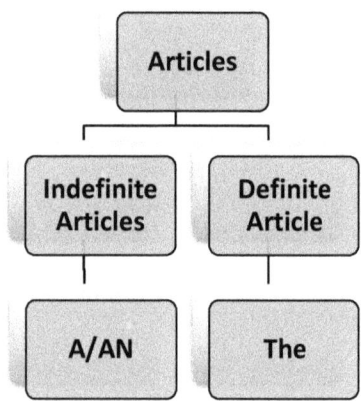

(1) **Indefinite Articles :** 'A' or 'An' is used to uncertain (Indefinite) the position of a noun :
1. He saw an old man.
2. There was a king
3. A dog was barking at night

(2) **Definite Article :** 'The' is used to certain the position of a noun :
1. The house in which I live is new
2. This is the pen which I have bought.
3. The gold of Nepal is cheap

Position of Articles

Rule - (1) 'A', 'An' or 'The' Takes its position before noun, as

      art.   N

e.g. I have <u>a book</u>

Rule - (2) It an adjective is used before a noun

    art.   Adj   N

e.g. : she is <u>an</u> <u>intelligent</u> <u>girl</u>.

Rule - (3) If an adverb is used before adjective + noun

    art   adv.   Adj.   N

e.g. : she is <u>a very</u> <u>intelligent</u> <u>girl</u>.

    Art.   Adv.   Adj.   N

He is <u>the</u> <u>very</u> <u>best</u> <u>player</u>.

Rule - (4) If 'such', 'what', 'many' etc. is used/ placed before a singular noun

eg: (1) such a girl   (correct)
      A such girl   (wrong)
   (2) Many a book   (correct)
      Many a books   (wrong)

Note: There are 20 vowel sounds in English alphabet.

Vowels :		(Phonetics)	
1.	iː	(ई)	as in three
2.	I	(इ)	as in city
3.	e	(ए)	as in bed
4.	ae	(ऐ)	as in cat
5.	aː	(आ)	as in car
6.	a	(ओ)	as in cot
7.	ɔː	(ऑ)	as in law
8.	uː	(ऊ)	as in food
9.	u	(उ)	as in book
10.	ɜː	(अः)	as in earth
11.	ʌ	(अ)	as in cup
12.	ə	(अ)	as in ego
13.	er	(ए)	as in day
14.	ar	(आइ)	as in time
15.	ɔp	(आई)	as in boy
16.	əu	(ओ)	as in old
17.	au	(आउ)	as in town
18.	Iə	(इअ)	as in deer
19.	eə	(एअ)	as in care
20.	uə	(उअ)	as in poor

Note: There are twenty four (24) consonant sounds in English.

Consonants :

ENGLISH

1.	p	(प)	as in pen
2.	b	(ब)	as in ball
3.	t	(ट)	as in ten
4.	d	(ड)	as in day
5.	k	(क)	as in cat
6.	g	(ग)	as in gun
7.	H	(च)	as in child
8.	d3	(ज)	as in judge
9.	f	(फ)	as in fan
10.	v	(व)	as in van
11.	φ	(थ)	as in thumb
12.	ð	(द)	as in they
13.	s	(स)	as in sun
14.	z	(ज)	as in zoo
15.	ʃ	(श)	as in shoe
16.	ʒ	(ज)	as in pleasure
17.	h	(ह)	as in hen
18.	m	(म)	as in man
19.	n	(न)	as in not
20.	ŋ	(न्ग)	as in ring
21.	l	(ल)	as in leg
22.	r	(र)	as in room
23.	j	(य)	as in yes
24.	w	(व)	as in wife

Note:- If the first letter of a word is consonant and its first sound is vowel like a, aa, i, ee, u, oo, e, ai, o, au/ou etc. of Hindi vowel, An is used before the word: as like

1. An honest man
2. An M.A
3. An M.L.A
4. An NCC boy
5. An honors
6. An X-mas tree
7. An H.M.T watch
8. A L.P. School

Note:- If the first letter of a word is vowel and its first sound is consonant like - k, kn, g, ----- h etc. of Hindi consonants 'A' is used before the word

1. A European
2. A university
3. A uniform
4. A utensil
5. A unanimous decision
6. A one-eyed girl
7. A union
8. A unit
9. A unique dress
10. A useful cow
11. A one- rupee note
12. A one-way ticket

Note:- When you have confusion about the sounds of English letters. You will not use 'A' or 'An' correctly

(a) A wooden table (वुडेन टेबुल)   (√)
(b) An wooden table (ऊडेन टेबुल)   (x)
(c) A year (यिअर)   (√)
(d) A year (ईअर)   (x)

Some more example

A and An is used in these phrases;

A team of	An army of
A gang of	An assembly of
A crowd of	Keep an appointment
A pair of	Make an excuse
A flock of	Have an opportunity

SUBJECT VERB AGREEMENT

The subject and the verb in a sentence must always agree. It the subject is singular, this verb must be singular, and if the subject is plural, the verb must also be plural

Rules of subject - verb Agreement

Rule- 1

When we make a sentence, we tell something about a person or a thing. The part of the sentence which names the person or a thing is called the 'subject' and the part which gives as more information about the subject is called the 'predicate' of the sentence.

A subject can be :

Singular - a book, an egg, a key

Plural - women, boys, flowers

uncountable - sugar, water, furniture

Rule- 2

GRAMMAR ARTICLES

Two or more singular subjects if joined together take a plural verb.

e.g: gold and silver are precious metals.

Rule- 3 Nouns plural in form, but singular in meaning take a plural verb.

e.g: compasses, tongs, trousers

Rule- 4 when a plural noun comes between a singular subject and its verb the verb agrees with the singular subject.

e.g.: Neither of the students was involved.

SUBJECT-VERB AGREEMENT

Exercise & practice with Explanation

(1) Choose the correct form of the verb that agrees with the subject:

1. His pants _____ torn during the match.
   - (a) was   [ ]
   - (b) is   [ ]
   - (c) were   [ ]
   - (d) are   [ ]

2. Arun, together with his wife _____ the guests of the party.
   - (a) greets   [ ]
   - (b) greet   [ ]
   - (c) greeting   [ ]
   - (d) are greeting [ ]

3. Tweezers _____ always useful to handle small objects
   - (a) may   [ ]
   - (b) is   [ ]
   - (c) will [ ]
   - (d) are   [ ]

4. The jury _____ not convinced.
   - (a) might [ ]
   - (b) was   [ ]
   - (c) were   [ ]
   - (d) would [ ]

5. The truthful _____ always trustworthy.
   - (a) is   [ ]
   - (b) was [ ]
   - (c) are [ ]
   - (d) may [ ]

6. To cry _____ never the solution to any problems
   - (a) are   [ ]
   - (b) were   [ ]
   - (c) should [ ]
   - (d) is   [ ]

7. A number of soldiers _____ injured during the war
   - (a) is   [ ]
   - (b) were [ ]
   - (c) was   [ ]
   - (d) might [ ]

8. The number of decreased soldiers _____ not stared in the record book.
   - (a) were [ ]
   - (a) are [ ]
   - (c) is   [ ]
   - (d) may [ ]

9. A pack of lions _____ approaching the camp.
   - (a) will [ ]
   - (b) were [ ]
   - (c) are   [ ]
   - (d) was   [ ]

10. Killing _____ not always considered a bad thing.
    - (a) were   (b) are
    - (c) was   (d) would

11. There _____ many difficulties regarding the situation
    - (a) should (b) was
    - (c) were   (d) is

12. Here _____ the tomb of Albert Einstein.
    - (a) lies   (b) lie
    - (c) lying   (d) lied

13. Either she or her friends _____ responsible for this accident.
    - (a) is   (b) are
    - (c) was   (d) might

ENGLISH

PARTS OF SPEECH (NOUN)

Noun:- A Noun is the name of person, place thing, quality, condition and action Like

Person	-	Raj
Place	-	Kota
Thing	-	Pen
Quality	-	Honesty
Condition	-	Illness
Action	-	movement

Noun
- Countable Noun
  - Proper Noun
  - Common Noun
  - Collective Noun
- Uncountable Noun
  - Abstract Noun
  - Material Noun

(1) **Countable Noun :** The Nouns which can be counted as, veena girl, class etc.

(a) **Proper Noun :** The Noun which denotes a proper person, place or thing as,
proper person - Raju, Ajit, Nilam
proper place - Mumbai, Kolkata, Delhi
proper thing - Ramayana, gita, Bible

(b) **Common Noun :** The common Noun which denotes common person, places or things as
Common person -Man, woman
Common Place - Town, School
Common things - Book, Table

(c) **Collective Noun :** The Noun which denotes a group of persons or other creatures and collection of things as.

Group of persons	A crew of sailors
	A team of players
	A class of students
	An army of soldiers
Collection of things	A fleet of ships
	A bunch of flowers
	A library of books

(a) **Material Noun :** The Noun which denotes materials as copper, silver tea, ghee, cotton etc

(b) **Abstract Noun :** The Noun which denotes quality, condition or action. as wisdom, humanity, pride, bravery, childhood etc.

Some important collective Nouns

(1) A crowd of people
(2) A herd of cattle
(3) A gang of robbers
(4) A she of of grains
(5) A galaxy of stars
(6) A course of study
(7) A flights of locusts
(8) A wardrobe of clothes
(9) A heap of stone
(10) A stock of coal

PRONOUN

Pronoun :-

Pronoun means for a noun. A pronoun is a word used instead of a Noun :
e.g : Ram is a handsome boy.
He is my student.

Note : Generally you know that a pronoun is used to stop the repetition of a noun. If we use a noun in a sentence again and again. The beauty of sentence ends.
This is main reason that a pronoun is used instead of noun.

Kinds of pronoun

(1) Personal Pronouns : I , me, we, as, you, he, him, she, her, it they them.
(2) Possessive Pronouns : Mine, ours, yours his, hers, theirs.
(3) Demonstrative Pronouns : This, That, These Those, such
(4) Distributive Pronouns : Each, Either, Neither
(5) Reciprocal Pronouns : Each other, one another
(6) Reflexive Pronouns : Myself, ourselves your self, yourselves himself, itself, themselves, oneself It also called Emphatic

(7) **Indefinite Pronouns :** Everybody, somebody, Nobody, Anybody, Everyone, Someone, No one, Anyone, Everything, Something Nothing, Anything, all, some, any, both, another, much, few, little

(8) **Relative Pronouns :** who, whom, whose, which, that.

(9) **Interrogative Pronouns:** when the pronouns - 'who', 'whom', 'whose', which and 'what' are used to ask a question. These are called Interrogative pronouns.

(10) **Exclamatory Pronouns :** When the Pronoun 'what is used to express 'sense of surprise' then it is called an exclamatory pronoun.

Personal Pronouns

Those pronouns which are used in three person such as First person, Second person and 'third person' are called personal pronouns

Persons	Singular Number	Plural Number
(1) First Person	I	We
(2) Second person	You	You
(3) Third person	He/She/it	They

First Person –

Those pronouns which denote a speaker are called the pronouns of first person.

➤ Singular- I - me - my - mine
➤ Plural - we - us - our - ours

Eg : I am a Teacher   You love me
This is my book   That book is mine
We are active   They help us
our country is great   These pens are ours

Second Person-

Those pronouns which denote an audience are called pronouns of second person.

➤ Singular - you - you - your - yours
➤ Plural - you - you - your - yours

Eg : you are hard worked
I love you.
This book is yours
This is your book.

Third Person - Those pronouns which denote the persons or things spoken of are called the pronouns of third person.

➤ Singular - He (masculire) - him - his - his
She (feminine) - her - her - hers
it (Neuter) - it - its - its

➤ Plural - they - them – their - theirs

Eg :   He loves you
She hates you/me
you admire him
They read in this school.
Those ball are theirs
Do you know them?

DISTRIBUTIVE PRONOUN

Those Pronouns which are used to denote one different from two or more than two persons or things are called Distributive pronouns e.g. Each, Either, Neither.

(1) Each of the boys won a prize
(2) Neither of these two girls is active
(3) Either of these two pens is red.

➤ **Rule (1) The Distributive Pronoun** - 'each' is used in the sense of 'every' for two or more than two persons or things as,
E.g - Each of the two students was honest

➤ **Rule (2) The Distributive Pronoun** - 'Either' is used in the sense of 'one of the two for two persons or things but not for more than two persons or things
E.g - Either of us can do it.

➤ **Rule (3) The Distributive Pronoun** - 'Neither' is used in the sense of 'Not one of the two' for two persons or things, But not for more than two persons or things
E.g - Neither of our hands is damaged

➤ **Rule (4)** 'Both' is used for two persons or things
E.g : Both of the two students are careless.

ENGLISH

3. RECIPROCAL PRONOUN

'Each other' and 'one another' are called Reciprocal Pronouns because they express reciprocal relationship.

E.g.: The two girls love
each other.
we all love one-another.
They are ready to go there.

4. REFLEXIVE PRONOUN

The pronouns ending with self or selves are called Reflexive Pronouns. These reflexive pronouns are also called self-pronouns.

such as – My self, ourselves, yourself, yourselves, himself, herself, itself themselves.

➤ **Difference between Reflexive and Emphasizing Pronouns**

Reflexive Pronouns	Emphasizing Pronouns
1. Reflexive Pronouns are used in the sense of 'self	(1) While Emphasizing Pronouns are also used in the sense of 'self'
2. If A person or a thing is the subject and object of a verb in a sentence, Reflexive Pronouns are used as an object of the verb, as e.g Ram ruined himself	(2) Emphasizing pronouns are not used as an object of the ver. But Emphasizing pronouns are used as an object of the preposition as He lives in this house by himself.
3. Reflixe Pronouns are not used as subjects e.g Myself saw it (×) I saw it (√)	(3) Emphasizing pronouns are also not used as subject Myself saw it (×) I myself saw it (√)

Remember :

(1) **The Reflexive Pronoun** - himself is used for masculine words - Ram, Krishna, Rajeev, The boy, father, brother etc.

(2) **The Reflexive Pronoun** - 'herself' is used for feminine words - sita, Richa the girl, mother, sister etc.

(3) **The Singular Reflexive Pronoun** - 'himself' and plural Reflexive Pronoun - 'themselves' are used for the nouns of common gender such as - the doctor, the teacher, the engineer etc in singular or plural sense respectively. But the singular reflexive pronoun 'herself' is used to denote female.

(4) **The Reflexive Pronoun** - 'oneself' is used for an Indefinite Pronoun- 'one'

(5) **The Singular Reflexive Pronoun** - himself is used for the pronouns of common gender such as - everyone, someone, anyone, no one, everybody, somebody, anybody, nobody but the singular reflexive pronoun - herself' is used to denote female.

Note: The nouns of common gender - Child, infant, baby do not signify the sex- male female. The singular pronoun and Adjective- it, itself and 'its' are used for the nouns of common gender - child, Infant, baby.

The reflexive pronoun - 'itself' is used for them.

e.g : The baby cried itself.
It was beautiful.
The baby has broken its leg.

Note: If the same person or thing is the subject and object of a verb in a sentence, The Reflexive Pronouns are used as an object of the verb : as.

1.	I hurt my self	(√)
	I hurt mineself	(×)
2.	we hurt ourselves	(√)
	we hurt ourself	(×)
3.	you hurt yourself (singular)	(√)
	you hurt yourself	(×)
4.	He hurts himself	(√)
	He hurts himselves	(×)
5.	One hurts oneself	(√)
	One hurts oneselves	(×)

5. DEMONSTRATIVE PRONOUN

Those pronouns which are used to point out or demonstrate the person or things, are called Demonstrative pronouns such as -

This, That, These, Those, Such.

Demonstrative Pronoun	Demonstrative Adjectives
1. Demonstrative Pronouns are used for nouns. They are not used before nouns, This is a gift from her. That is just what he wants.	(1) Demonstrative Adjectives are used before nouns. E.g. Those men were not present in that place. (2) These flowers are mine

➢ **Rule (1) The demonstrative Pronoun** - This is used for a person or a thing that is nearest to the speaker, while the demonstrative pronoun These is used for more than one person or thing that is nearest to the speaker. E.g. This is a cat (Singular)
    These are cats (Plural)

➢ **Rule (2) The demonstrative Pronoun** - 'That' is used for a person or a thing that is distant or farther away to the speaker, while (whereas) The demonstrative Pronouns 'those' is used for more than one person or thing that is distant or farther away to the speaker as
E.g That is a book (Singular)
    Those are books (Plural)

➢ **Rule (3)** If two singular nouns are joined by 'and' and used in a sentence or a clause, the demonstrative pronoun 'This' is used for the last singular noun and the demonstrative pronoun - 'that' is used for the first singular noun.
as'-

E.g work and play are both necessary to health; This (= play) exercises the body, and that (= work) exercises the brain.

➢ **Rule (4)** It two plural nouns are joined by 'an' and used in a sentence or a clause, the demonstrative pronoun- 'These' is used for the last plural noun and the demonstrative pronoun - 'Those' is used for the first plural noun as -
E.g. Cows and horses are both useful these (= horses) carry as from one place to another, and those (= cows) give us milk.

➢ **Rule (5) The demonstrative Pronoun** - 'such' is used both in singular and plural sense
E.g. He is the house owner and as such he has the right to maintain the house.
(such =The house owner)
Criminals are restricted such by law. (such = criminals) such is your mistake that nobody can forgive you.

Note: If 'such' is used before a noun, that is called Demonstrative Adjective Like : Nobody can forgive you for such a mistake.

6. Indefinite Pronoun

Those pronouns which denote Indefinite persons or things are called Indefinite pronouns.

E.g. : everybody, somebody, nobody, anybody, everyone, someone, no one, anyone, everything, something, nothing anything, all, some, both, any most enough, few, many, none, little others These are also called indefinite demonstrative pronouns.

E.g. :

(1) One must be alternative to one's studies.
(2) Everyone believed him.
(3) Somebody has stolen my watch.

(4) <u>Nobody</u> was there to save the drawing child.

(5) <u>Some</u> are born great. All are not born rich.

(6) <u>Few</u> were hurt, many escaped

(7) <u>All</u> that glitters is not gold.

(8) Only Rakesh can remain here, <u>others</u> may go home

(9) <u>One</u> or <u>Other</u> of us will be there.

In the sentences given above, The underlined pronouns have been used to denote Indefinite persons or things. So these are not used to denote definite persons or things.

Note: The words - all, some, both, any, most, enough, few, many, little, one, other another are generally used as adjectives.

E.g.: I will take you there <u>one</u> day.

<u>Any</u> fool can do that.

He is a man of <u>few</u> words

<u>Some</u> milk was spilt.

<u>Many</u> Criminals were arrested.

7. RELATIVE PRONOUN

Those pronouns which denote relation to the nouns or noun equivalent words used before themselves and function to join two sentences are called Relative Pronouns. They function as conjunctions. So, They are also called Connective pronouns or conjunctions. Such as- who, which, that, as, but, what.

Look at these sentences:

I met Veena, <u>who</u> was returning from school.

Nilu had a book, <u>which</u> she bought at a shop.

The pen <u>that</u> my father gave writes well.

In the sentences given above, The words- 'who', 'which' and 'that' denote relation to the nouns- 'Veena',' a book' and 'the pen' used before themselves respectively and function to join the two sentences. So, These are relative pronouns.

Antecedent : The noun or noun equivalent word (= pronoun) used before relative pronouns (=who, which, that... etc.) is called Antecedent.

Function of Relative Pronouns in Subordinate Clause:

Rule (1): The Relative Pronouns - who/which/that are used as the subject of a subordinate clause; as,

The boy <u>who</u> came here is a player.

This is the house <u>which</u> is made of marbles.

The road <u>that</u> leads to Patna market is being repaired.

In the sentences given above, the relative pronouns- 'who', 'which' and 'that' have been used as the subjects of the subordinate clauses.

Rule (2): The Relative Pronouns - whom, which and that are used as the object of a verb in a subordinate clause; as,

I have a son <u>whom</u> I <u>love</u> very much.

This is the house <u>which</u> my father <u>built</u>.

The sewing machine <u>that</u> I borrowed <u>broke down</u> yesterday.

In the sentences given above, the Relative Pronoun- whom, which and that have been used as the objects of the verbs in the subordinate clauses.

Rule (3): The Relative Pronouns are used as the object of a preposition in a subordinate clause; as, The cut <u>on</u> <u>which</u> I was sitting began to creak.

This is the pen <u>with which</u> we usually write.

She is the girl <u>with whom</u> I lived.

In the sentences given above, The Relative Pronouns- which, which and whom have been used as the object of the prepositions- on, with and with in the subordinate clauses.

PRACTICE SET – 7

Based on Relative Pronouns:

Q.1 Pick out the relative pronouns in the following sentences, tell the case of each, and mention its antecedent:

1. We met the girls who were rewarded.
2. Bring me the letters which the postman left.
3. The students who were lazy were punished.
4. The pen that you gave me is a very good one.
5. The answer which you gave is not right.
6. They also serve who only stand and wait.
7. He knows the woman whose child was hurt.
8. Here is the book that you lent me.
9. This is the house that Jack built.
10. Mr. Thakur hates the children who throw stone at birds.
11. He has not brought the book that I asked for.
12. Vikas saw the man who had been hurt.
13. This is the beggar whom we saw yesterday.
14. The cat killed the rat that ate the corn.
15. Show me the mobile set that you have bought.
16. We met the sailors whose ship was wrecked.
17. The flowers which grow in our garden are not for sale.
18. He that is contented is happy.
19. They that seek wisdom will be wise.
20. The moment which is lost is lost for ever.

Q.2 Fill in the blanks with suitable relative pronouns :

1. This is the beggar....... stole my suitcase.
2. I, ... am your teacher, will teach you.
3. This is the horse...... won the race.
4. I don't believe ...... you say.
5. He plays the game ..... he likes best.
6. My uncle, ... I loved, is dead.
7. They always talk .... never think.
8. They .... touch pitch will be defiled.
9. I gave it to the man ..... I saw there.
10. He is a man ..... you can trust.
11. The answer .... she gave is wrong.
12. They never fail ..... die in a great cause.
13. The children .... were there were frightened.
14. It is only donkeys .... bray.
15. Man is the only animal .... can talk.
16. Such a man ...... he should be honoured.
17. God helps those ...... help themselves.
18. Do the same ..... I do.
19. Take anything ...... you like.
20. My answer is the same ...... yours (is).

Q.3 Correct the following sentences:

1. I met a man which was riding on an ass.
2. The girl whom is carrying the basket is my classmate.
3. This is the man that son stood first.
4. He prayeth best whom loveth best.
5. I know cats which intelligence is almost equal to men's.
6. My old horse, which is faithful to me, has more sense than most men.
7. The time who is once lost is lost forever.
8. The dog who bit him has been shot.
9. He is the best speaker whom I ever heard.

ENGLISH

10. Who is here who does not love his country.
11. Who am I whom I should object.
12. Man is the only animal who laughs.
13. You may take any pen which you like.
14. He is the same man who came here yesterday.
15. All which glitters is not gold.
16. It was not for nothing which he spent five years studying medicine.
17. He gave me just that I deserved.
18. Listen carefully to whom I say.
19. She found which she was looking for.
20. He is not such a clever student that you are.

Q.4 *Find out the error part of the following sentences:*

1. The man (1)/who they thought (2)/to be a gentleman (3)/is a rouge. (4)/ No error (5)
2. This is (1)/one of the best suggestions (2)/which have ever been (3)/made by you. (4)/No error (5)
3. This is (1)/the only one of his comments (2)/that (3)/deserve our attention. (4)/No error (5)
4. This is (1)/ not such treatment (2)/that (3)/I expected. (4)/No error (5)
5. May I (1)/know (2)/who you want (3)/to see please? (4)/No error (5)
6. A woman can do (1) / everything (2) / what a man (3) / can do. (4) / No error (5)
7. She told him that (1) / she didn't want to marry him, (2)/ what in my opinion (3) / was very silly of her. (4) / No error (5)
8. Those applicants (1)/ which the selection committee recommends (2)/ for interview (3) / should be contacted without delay. (4) / No error (5)
9. She is (1) / one of the few people (2)/ whom I think (3)/ might be good at the job. (4) / No error (5)
10. Students (1) / which fail in the exam (2) / have to take (3)/ the course again. (4) No error (5)
11. Mr. Thakur (1) / likes music (2) / who helps me (3) to relax. (4) / No error. (5)
12. Whomever (1) / will violate (2) / these rules of law (3) / shall be punished. (4) / No error (5)
13. I will (1) / take with me (2)/ whosoever (3) / you choose. (4) / No error (5)
14. There is (1) / no man (2) / who knows (3) / these things. (4) / No error (5)
15. What (1) / is there (2)/that (3) /I do not know? (4)/ No error (5)
16. I hate (1)/ everybody and everything who (2) / reminds me (3)/of my mistakes. (4) / No error (5)
17. The terrorist (1)/which was chained (2) /grumble at the D.S.P. (3)/who was taking him to prison. (4) / No error (5)
18. This is the same (1)/dog which barked (2)/ at my son but fortunately did not (3)/bite him. (4)/No error (5)
19. I (1)/ don't like (2)/that you told (3) my mother last night. (4)/No error (5)
20. Don't respect (1)/ such persons (2)/ who have no respect (3)/for elders. (4)/No error (5)

ANSWERS WITH EXPLANATION

Q.1.

1. 'Who' is the relative pronoun of nominative case and its antecedent is *the girls*.
2. 'Which' is the relative pronoun of objective case and its antecedent is *the letters*.
3. 'Who' is the relative pronoun of nominative case and its antecedent is *the students*.
4. 'That' is the relative pronoun of objective case and its antecedent is *the pen*.
5. 'Which' is the relative pronoun of objective case and its antecedent is *the answer*.
6. 'Who' is the relative pronoun of nominative case and the personal pronoun- *they* functions as its antecedent.
7. 'Whose' is a possessive relative pronoun and its antecedent is *the woman*.
8. 'That' is the relative pronoun of objective case and its antecedent is *the book*.
9. 'That' is the relative pronoun of objective case and its antecedent is *the house*.
10. 'Who' is the relative pronoun of nominative case and its antecedent is *the children*.
11. 'That' is the relative pronoun of objective case and its antecedent is *the book*.
12. 'Who' is the relative pronoun of nominative case and its antecedent is *the man*.
13. 'Whom' is the relative pronoun of objective case and its antecedent is *the beggar*.
14. 'That' is the relative pronoun of nominative case and its antecedent is *the rat*.
15. 'That' is the relative pronoun of objective case and its antecedent is *the mobile set*.
16. 'Whose' is the relative pronoun of possessive case and its antecedent is *the sailors*.
17. 'Which' is relative pronoun of nominative case and its antecedent is *the flowers*.
18. 'That' is the relative pronoun of nominative case and its antecedent is *he*. The word *contented* is an adjective.
19. 'That' is the relative pronoun of nominative case and its antecedent is *they*.
20. 'Which' is the relative pronoun of nominative case and its antecedent is *the moment*.

Q.2

1. Who/that
2. who
3. which
4. what
5. which
6. whom
7. who
8. that/who
9. whom
10. that/ whom
11. which/that
12. who
13. who
14. that
15. that
16. as
17. who
18. as
19. that
20. as

Q.3.

1. I met a man who was riding on an ass.
2. the girl who is carrying the basket is my classmate.
3. This is the man whose son stood first.
4. He prayed best who loveth best.
5. I know cats whose intelligence is almost equal to men's.
6. My old horse, who is faithful to me, has more sense than most men.

ENGLISH

7. The time which is once lost is lost forever.
8. The dog which bit him has been shot.
9. He is the best speaker that I ever heard.
10. Who is here that does not love his country.
11. Who am I that I should object.
12. Man is the only animal that laughs.
13. You may take any pen that you like.
14. He is the same man that came here yesterday.
15. All that litters is not gold.
16. It was not fore nothing that he spent five years studying medicine.
17. He gave me just what I deserved.
18. Listen carefully to what I say.
19. She found what she was looking for.
20. He is not such a clever student as you are.

Q.4.

1. (2) The relative pronoun-*'whom'* will be used in place of the relative pronoun-*'who'*.
2. (3) The relative pronoun-*'that'* will be used in place of the relative pronoun- *'which'*.
3. (4) The singular verb-*'deserves'* will be used in place of the plural verb-*'deserve'*. The Relative Pronoun-*'that'* is used after the structure-*'the only one of + Possessive Adjective + plural noun'* and A singular verb is used with it (=the relative pronoun-*'that'*).
4. (3) The relative pronoun-*'As'* will be used in place of the relative pronoun-'that' because the word-*'As'* is used as a relative pronoun after the word-*'such'*.
5. (3) The relative pronoun- *'whom'* will be used in place of the relative pronoun-*'who'*.
6. (3) the relative pronoun-*'that'* will be used in place of the relative pronoun-*'what'*.
7. (3) The relative pronoun- *'which'* will be used in place of the relative pronoun-*'what'*.
8. (2) The Relative Pronoun-*'whom'* will be used in place of the relative pronoun -*'which'*.
9. (3) The relative pronoun-*'who'* or *'that'* will be used in place of the Relative Pronoun-*'whom'*. The Relative Pronoun- *'who'* or 'that' is used as nominative relative pronoun for person.
10. (2) The relative pronoun - *'who'* or 'that' will be used in place of the relative pronoun-*'which'*.
11. (3) The relative pronoun - *'which'* or 'that' will be used in place of the relative pronoun-*'who'*
12. (1) The compound relative pronoun-*'whomsoever'* will be used in place of the compound relative pronoun-*'whomever'*
13. (3) The compound relative pronoun-*'whomsoever'* will be used in place of the compound relative pronoun-*'whosoever'*.
14. (3) The relative pronoun- *'but'* will be used in place of the relative pronoun-*'who'*. The word-'but' is used in the sense of *'who... not'* or 'which...not' as a relative pronoun after a negative word. Here *'but'* means *'who dose not'*. 'But' is suitable for the meaning of the given sentence.
15. (5) Given sentence is correct because the relative pronoun-*'that'* is used after the interrogative word-*'what'*.
16. (2) The relative pronoun- *'that'* will be used in place of the relative pronoun-*'who'*
17. (2) The relative pronoun-*'who'* will be used in place of the relative pronoun-*'which'*.
18. (2) The relative pronoun- *'that'* will be used in place of (= explained/ obvious), The Relative pronoun-*'that'* is used after *'the same'*.
19. (3) The relative pronoun-*'what'* will be used in place of the relative pronoun-*'that'*.
20. (3) The relative pronoun-'what' will be used in place of the relative pronoun-*'who'*. The relative pronoun- *'As'* is used after the word-*'such'*.

ADJECTIVES

Adjective: An Adjective is a word used to qualify a Noun or Pronoun. *Or, Qualifying words are known* as Adjectives.

as,
1. She is a beautiful woman.
2. Ajit is handsome and intelligent.
3. He has a big house.
4. It is a charming scenery.
5. He is rich.

In the sentences given above, The words-beautiful, handsome and intelligent, big, charming and rich have been used to qualify the nouns-woman, Ajit, house, scenery and the pronoun-'*he*'. So, these are Adjectives.

Use o Adjectives

There are two uses of Adjectives:

1. **Attributive use:** When an adjective is used before a noun, such use of an adjective is called Attributive use; as,
   1. He has a red Pen.
   2. He was an intelligent man.

   In the sentences given above, The Adjectives-red and intelligent have been used before the nouns-pen and man respectively. Such use of Adjectives is called Attributive use.

2. **Predicative use:** When an adjective is not used before a noun or when an adjective is used to qualify the noun or pronoun used as the subject in the Predicative part of the sentence. Such use of an adjective is called predicative use; as,
   1. She was industrious.
   2. Maheshwar Babu is intelligent.

   In the sentences given above, The adjectives-'*industrious*' and '*intelligent*' have been used in the predicative part of the given sentence which qualifies the pronoun-'*she*' and the noun - Maheshwar Babu used as the subject of the sentence. Such use of Adjectives is called Predicative use.

Note: Study the Attributive use and predicative use in the table given below:

Attributive use (Adj. + N)	Predicative use
1. Raju is an honest boy.	1. Raju is honest.
2. He was a laborious man.	2. He was laborious.
3. America has a big army.	3. America is big.
4. This is a red book.	4. This book is red.

KINDS OF ADJECTIVE

1. **Adjective of quality or qualitative Adjective-** good, bad, red, black, tall, short, beautiful, ugly, long.........etc.

2. **Adjective of quantity or quantitative Adjective-** some, any, no, little, much, all, whole, enough, sufficient, none, most........etc.

3. **Adjective of number or Numeral Adjectives -** one, two, three, ...etc.
   Next, last, first, second, third, ... etc, Many, few, various, some, all, sufficient, no, none, most, whole, enough, several, ...etc.

4. **Proper Adjective-** Indian, American, Chinese, Japanese, Nepalese, Russian ......etc.

5. **Possessive Adjective-** My, our, your, his, her, its, their.

6. **Distributive Adjective-** each, every, either, neither.

7. **Demonstrative Adjective-** This, that these, those, such, the same, some, any, a certain, certain, any other, other, another.

8. **Interrogative Adjective-** what, which, whose.

9. **Emphasizing Adjective or Emphatic Adjective-** own, very.

10. **Exclamatory Adjective-** what.

ENGLISH

DEFINITION OF THE KINDS OF ADJECTIVE

1. **Adjectives of quality:** The Adjectives which denote/show the colour, shape, size, kind, quality (merits-demerits), state/ condition of a person or thing are called Adjectives of quality; as
   1. Raman is a tall man.
   2. He is a foolish student.
   3. She is a beautiful girl.
   4. I write with an old pen.

   In the sentences given above, The Adjectives- tall, foolish, beautiful and old have been used before the nouns-man, student, girl and pen respectively-which qualifies them (the nouns- man, students, girl and pen); and also show the quality-tallness, foolishness, beauty and oldness of the nouns-man, students, girl and pen respectively.

   Note: Adjective of quality answer the question : *'of what kind?'*

2. **Adjectives of quantity :** The Adjectives which denote/ show the quantity of a thing are called Adjectives of quantity. They tell us how much of a thing is meant/intended.
   e.g. A good deal of, A great deal of, A large amount of, A large quantity of, a lot of, lots of, plenty of, a part of, half of, ...etc; as,
   e.g. Mukesh has enough money. He has lost all his wealth. She has a lot of coffee.
   There is a little water in the glass.
   In the sentences given above, The Adjectives - enough, all, a lot of and a little have been used before the nouns- money, wealth, coffee and water respectively which show/denote their quantity.

   Note: Adjectives of quantity answer the question: *'How much?'* .

3. **Adjectives of Number :** The Adjectives which show/ denote the number of persons or things are called Adjectives of number. They show how many of *'In what order persons or things are meant/taken or stand'*; as,
   I have three rooms.
   The two sisters have left for London.
   There are forty students in the class.
   Binay is the second son of Mr. Maheshwar Thakur.
   Many criminals were killed.
   In the the sentences given above, The Adjectives-three, two, forty, second and many have been used before the nouns-rooms, sisters, students, son and criminals respectively which show/denote their number (= definite/Indefinite), order (=sequence).

4. **Proper Adjectives :** The Adjectives which are formed from proper nouns are called Proper Adjectives, such as-
   Remember:

Proper Nouns	Proper Adjectives	Proper Nouns	Proper Adjectives
China	Chinese	Nepal	Nepalese
Switzerland	Swiss	Portugal	Portuguese
Israel	Israeli	Pakistan	Pakistani
Africa	African	Australia	Australian
Canada	Canadian	Germany	German
Greece	Greek	India	Indian
Italy	Italian	Russia	Russian
Asia	Asian	England	English
France	French	Holland	Dutch
Brazil	Brazilian	Britain	British, etc.

   Note: Proper Nouns or Proper Adjectives are always written in capital __ letter. In other words, The first letter of a proper noun or Proper Adjective is capital.

5. **Possessive Adjectives:** Ownership denoting Adjectives (such as - my, our, your, his, her, its,

their) are called Possessive Adjectives. These are always used before nouns; as,

This is your pen. That is my car,

These are our chairs.

These are his books.

In the sentences given above, The Adjectives - your, my, our and his have been used before the nouns-pen, car, chairs and books respectively which denotes relationship or possession with them (= the nouns-pen, car, chairs and books)

In other words, Relationship or Possession expressing Adjectives are called Possessive Adjectives.

6. **Distributive Adjectives:** One or Each of the two or more than two persons or things denoting Adjectives are called Distributive Adjectives.

In other words, when the distribution expressing (=denoting) words-each, every, either and neither are used before nouns, these are called Distributive Adjectives. When the distribution expressing (- denoting/showing) words-each, either and neither are not used before nouns, these are called distributive pronouns; as,

Each girl has a book.
Every man is emotional.
Either book is yours.
Neither boy is handsome.

In the sentences given above, The Adjectives- each, every, either and neither have been used before the nouns-girl, man, book and boy respectively which denote each or one.

7. **Demonstrative Adjectives:** Demonstrating or pointing out persons or things denoting (=expressing) Adjectives are called Demonstrative Adjectives.

In other words, when pointing out persons or things expressing (=denoting) words such as- this, that, these, those, such, the same, some, any, a certain, certain any other, other and another are used before nouns are called demonstrative Adjectives.

When pointing out persons or things expressing (=denoting) words such as- this, that, these, those……. and another are not used before nouns are called demonstrative pronouns.

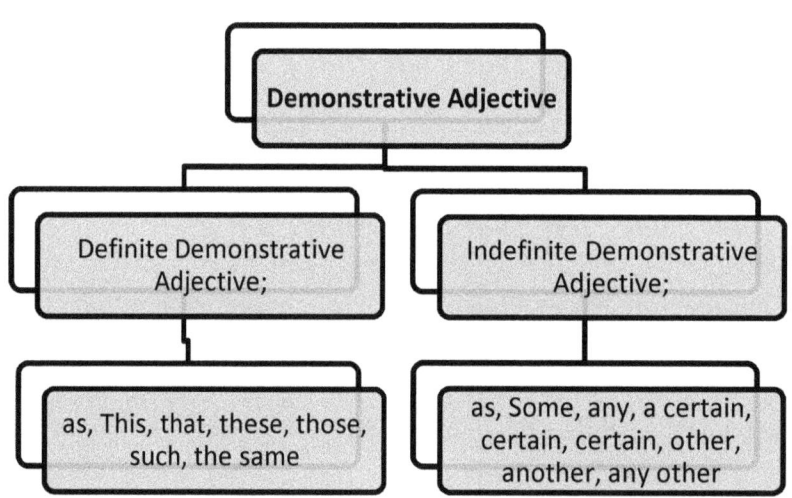

8. **Interrogative Adjectives :** The Adjectives which are used to ask a question are called Interrogative Adjectives such as-what, which and whose; These are used before nouns; as,

Which pen is yours?
Whose note book is this?
What book do you want to read?

In the sentences given above, The Adjectives- which, whose and what have been used before the nouns- pen, notebook and book respectively to ask questions. So, these are Interrogative Adjectives.

When the words-what, which, and whose are not used before nouns, these are called Interrogative pronouns.

9. **Emphasizing Adjectives:** When the words- own and very are used before nouns to emphasis them (the nouns), these are called Emphasizing Adjective; as,

He saw his beloved on the road with his own eyes.

She killed her husband before his very eyes.

In the sentence given above, The words-own and very have been used before the nouns- eyes and eyes to emphasis the nouns. So, these are emphasizing Adjectives.

10. **Exclamatory Adjectives:** When the word- 'what' is used to denote (=express) sense of surprise, This is called exclamatory Adjective; as,

What an ugly woman!

What a big building it is!

What a big fool!

In the sentences given above, The word-'*what*' has been used before the phrases- an ugly woman, a big building and a big fool to denote/express sense of surprise. So, this is an exclamatory Adjective.

DEGREES OF COMPARISON

There are three degrees of comparison in English
1. Positive degree   2. Comparative degree
3. Superlative degree

1. **Positive degree :** When an adjective is used to denote (express) common quality, condition/state, etc of a person o a thing, that adjective is in positive degree. The Adjective of positive degree is put in the middle of as ....as or so.......as. The pronoun of nominative case is used after '*As*'; as,

1. This table is heavy.
2. You are a good student.
3. Ramesh is as handsome as Suresh.
4. She is as beautiful as Veena.
5. He is not so good as I.

Note: '*As ....as*' or '*So..........as*' is used in Affirmative and negative sentence. But '*So.......as*' should be used in negative sentence because The use of '*So ....as*' is considered to be better in negative sentence.

2. **Comparative degree:** When an adjective is used to compare between the two persons or things, that Adjective is in comparative degree. The word-'*than*' is used after the Adjective/Adverb of comparative degree. The pronoun of nominative case is used after the word-'*than*'. If An Intransitive verb is used after the subject; as,

1. Mukesh is better than Pinku.
2. She is more beautiful than Shobhana.
3. He is taller than I.
4. America is richer than India.

The structure- 'The + Comparative degree + of the two + plural noun' is used to express the idea of selection; as,

She is the better of the two girls.

He was the more intelligent of the two boys.

Note: If A transitive verb is used after the subject; the pronoun of objective case is used after the word- '*than*'; as, You love him more than me.

3. **Superlative degree :** When an adjective is used to compare among the three or more than three persons or things (between more than two persons or things) and to express the highest degree of quality, that Adjective is in superlative degree; as,

Rani is the most beautiful girl in the class.

Rupkant Babu was the oldest man in the village.

He is the cleverest of all the three brothers.

Binay is the most intelligent student in the college.

➢ *Rules of forming (making) comparative degree and superlative degree form positive degree:*

Rule (1) : Generally comparative degree and superlative degree are formed (made) by adding 'er' and and 'est' respectively in the last of the Adjective of positive degree; as,

Positive degree	Comparative degree	Superlative degree
tall	Taller	tallest
high	Higher	highest
poor	Poorer	poorest
slow	Slower	slowest
bright	Brighter	brightest
great	Greater	greatest
dear	Dearer	dearest
clear	Clearer	clearest
cheap	Cheaper	cheapest
small	Smaller	smallest
long	Longer	longest
deep	Deeper	deepest
clever	Cleverer	cleverest
thick	Thicker	thickest
shallow	Shallower	shallowest
	more shallow	most shallow
rich	Richer	richest

Rule(2) : If 'e' is the last letter of the Adjective of Positive degree, comparative and superlative degree are formed (made) by adding only 'r' and 'st' respectively; as,

Positive degree	Comparative degree	Superlative degree
white	whiter	whitest
brave	braver	bravest
wise	wiser	wisest
wide	wider	widest
fine	finer	finest
able	abler	ablest
nice	nicer	nicest
large	larger	largest
noble	nobler	noblest
true	truer	truest

Rule(3): If the last letter (of the Adjective) of Positive degree, consonant and the consonant is preceded by vowel, The last letter-(the) consonant is doubled during the formation of comparative ad superlative degree by adding 'er' and 'est' respectively; as,

Positive degree	Comparative degree	Superlative degree
sad	sadder	saddest
red	redder	reddest
thin	thinner	thinnest
wet	wetter	wettest
hot	hotter	hottest
fit	fitter	fittest
fat	fatter	fattest
big	bigger	biggest
dim	dimmer	dimmest
slim	slimmer	slimmest

Rule(4) : If 'y' is the last letter (of the Adjective) of Positive degree, consonant and the 'y' is preceded by consonant, comparative adn superlative degree are formed by adding 'er' and 'est' respectively by changing the 'y' into 'i'; as,

Positive degree	Comparative degree	Superlative degree
easy	easier	easiest
lazy	lazier	laziest
heavy	heavier	heaviest
happy	happier	happiest
wealthy	wealthier	wealthiest
healthy	healthier	healthiest
dry	drier	driest
merry	merrier	merriest
pretty	prettier	prettiest
busy	busier	busiest
holy	holier	holiest

Rule(5): If 'y' is the last letter (of the Adjective) of Positive degree, and the 'y' is preceded by a vowel, comparative and superlative degree are formed by adding only 'er' and 'est' respectively. In this case, The 'y' is not changed into 'i'; as,

Positive degree	Comparative degree	Superlative degree
Gay (=delightful)	Gayer	Gayest
Grey (=brown)	Greyer	Greyest
Gray (=brown)	Grayer	Grayest

Rule (6): The comparative and superlative degree form of some adjectives of positives degree are different; as,

Positive degree	Comparative degree	Superlative degree
good	better	best
well	better	best
bad	worse	worst
ill	worse	worst
evil	worse	worst
fore	former	foremost, first
far (distance)	farther	farthest
late	later/latter	latest/last
little	less/lesser	least
much (quantity)	more	most
many (number)	more	most
nigh	nigher	nighest, next
old	older/elder	oldest/eldest
near	nearer	nearest
fore-Adverbs (movement)	further	furthest
in	inner	innermost
up	upper	uppermost
out	outer/utter	most, uttermost

Note: The words-'*Fore*', in, out and up are the adverbs which are in positive degree. Their comparative degree-Further, inner, outer/utter and upper are used as adjectives add their superlative degree-Furthest, innermost/in most, outermost/utmost and upper most are also used as adjectives.

Rule (7): The comparative and superlative degree are formed by adding '*more*' and '*most*' respectively to the head of the adjectives of the positive degree of two or more than two syllables; as,

Positive degree	Comparative degree	Superlative degree
difficult	more difficult	most difficult
laborious	more laborious	most laborious
intelligent	more intelligent	most intelligent
handsome	more handsome	most handsome (in current usage)
beautiful	more beautiful	most beautiful
interesting	more interesting	most interesting
expensive	more expensive	most expensive
courageous	more courageous	most courageous
magnificent	more magnificent	most magnificent
splendid	more splendid	most splendid
useful	more useful	most useful
famous	more famous	most famous
honest	more honest	most honest

Note: The comparative and superlative degree of the Adjective- '*handsome*' are '*handsomer*' and '*handsomer*' respectively. But they are not used in modern English.

VOCABULARY

PRACTICE SET

Q.1 Pick out the adjectives and state their kinds:
1. The coffee is not good.
2. The black cat caught a small bird.
3. The cow has a long tail.
4. Everyone makes several mistakes in his life.
5. He likes this pen.
6. How do you do this sum?
7. I like such a book.
8. Which is your pen?
9. A little boy was playing with his friends.
10. Which student broke this chair?
11. The spider has eight legs.
12. He wants some money.
13. All men are mortal.
14. A few students are present in the class.
15. Neither boy has come.
16. He likes the Nepalese tobacco.
17. He ate little bread.
18. A month has thirty days.
19. March is the third month of the year.
20. Each student has two pens.
21. Whose pen is this?
22. These apples are sweet.
23. The rose is a beautiful flower.
24. Man is a wonderful animal.
25. It was a glorious victory.

Q.2. Fill in the blank with suitable adjectives:
1. Lata is a ...... singer.
2. Which is the... day of the week?
3. We should always drink .... water.
4. Shakespeare wrote ... plays.
5. Dr. Rajendra Prasad was a ...... leader.
6. Patna is a ..... town.
7. That is a .....house.
8. Owls eat rats and ..... birds.
9. Who made .... shirt?
10. What is ...... name?
11. There is ...... water in the glass.
12. A ..... and ..... road runs to the station.
13. The hand has ..... fingers.
14. Quinine is bitter, but honey is ....
15. The days are hot, but the nights are ....
16. His ..... son is in the army.
17. Rahul was the ..... of the two brothers.
18. Mahatma Gandhi Setu is the ...... bridge in Asia.
19. The Taj Mahal is a ...... monument.
20. His ..... manners pleased us.
21. There are trees on ..... side of the road.
22. The Ramayana is a ..... book.
23. The ...... soldier fought bravely.
24. A..... knowledge is a dangerous thing.
25. He is ...... to see her.

Q.3 Fill in the blanks with suitable Adjectives given in the brackets:
1. There is not .... sugar in this pot now but there was ...... sugar in it yesterday
   (some, any)
2. There is not .... water in the well.
   (much, many)

ENGLISH

3. .... people think that there will be a war soon. **(much, many)**

4. I have ..... friends in Patna. **(a few, a little)**

5. I know ..... Bengali and less Hindi. **(little, a little)**

6. Mr. Yadav has ..... chance of being elected. **(little, a little)**

7. ...... villages in Bihar have dispensaries. **(few, a few)**

8. There are .... milk in the glass. **(some, any)**

9. There are ...... pens on the table. **(some, any)**

10. ..... guests came to see him this evening but he saw only..... **(a lot of, a few)**

11. Sometimes she put ...... salt in my vegetables. **(a few, a little)**

12. I had ...... work to do this morning but I could do only..... **(a lot of, a little)**

13. Binay has bought two pens, and ...... pen is black. **(each, every)**

14. A dog is a ...... animal. **(faithful, faithfully)**

15. There were trees on ..... side of the road. **(either, every)**

Q.4 *Fill in the blanks with suitable forms of Adjectives :*

Positive	Comparative	Superlative
1. much	....	....
2.	farther	....
3. hot	....	....
4.	....	least
5.	worse	....
6.	prettier	....
7. lucky	....	....
8. dirty	....	....
9. lovely	....	....
10.	drier	....
11.	....	shallowest
12.	cleverer	....
13. Noble	....	....
14. wide	....	....
15. fit	....	....
16. slim	....	....
17. merry	....	....
18.	busier	....
19. ill	....	....
20.	more	....
21.	inner	....
22.	upper	....
23.	....	utmost
24. late	....	....
25. Grey	....	....
26. Famous	....	....
27.	more honest	....
28. expensive	....	....
29.	....	most courageous
30. handsome	....	....
31. fast	....	....
32. badly	....	....
33. well	....	....
34. careful	....	....

#	Positive	Comparative	Superlative
35.	....	....	broadest
36.	sad	....	....
37.	....	younger	....
38.	....	older	....
39.	kind	....	....
40.	great	....	....
41.	close	....	....
42.	fond	....	....
43.	lazy	....	....
44.	fine	....	....
45.	....	bigger	....
46.	....	colder	....
47.	....	....	thickest
48.	....	....	widest
49.	....	thinner	....
50.	Tiny	....	....

Q.5 *Pick out the Adjectives and name the degree of comparison:*

1. Prabha is the most honest girl in the class.
2. No news is good news.
3. He congratulated me on my grand success.
4. This is the elder of the two sisters.
5. It was the happiest time of my life.
6. Lead is heavier than any other metal.
7. Love is greater than any other thing in the world.
8. A dead lion is not so good as a live ass.
9. She is not as beautiful as Gita.
10. Very few buildings in the world are so beautiful as the Taj Mahal.

ANSWERS WITH EXPLANATION

Q.1.
1. good-Adjective of quality
2. black-Adjective of quality
   small-Adjective of quality
3. small-Adjective of quality
   long-Adjective of quality
4. several-Adjective of quality
   his-Possessive Adjective
5. this-Demonstrative Adjective
6. this-Demonstrative Adjective
7. such-Demonstrative Adjective
8. your-Possessive Adjective
9. Little-is an adjective of quality because, little has been used in the sense of 'young' in the given sentence. Generally 'little' is and adjective of quantity.
   his-possessive adjective
10. which-Interrogative Adjective
    this-Demonstrative Adjective
11. eight-Adjective of number
12. some-Adjective of number
13. all-Adjective of number
14. A few- Adjective of number
15. Neither-Distributive Adjective
16. Nepalese-Proper Adjective
17. little-Adjective of quantity
18. thirty-Adjective of number (cardinal)
19. third-Adjective of number (ordinal)
20. Each-Distributive Adjective
21. whose-Interrogative Adjective
22. These-Demonstrative Adjective
23. beautiful-Adjective of quality
24. wonderful-Adjective of quality
25. glorious-Adjective of quality

Q.2.
1. famous
2. first/last
3. fresh
4. many
5. great
6. big
7. big
8. small
9. that
10. your/his/her
11. little
12. straight, wide
13. ten
14. sweet
15. cold
16. eldest
17. elder
18. longest
19. beautiful
20. good
21. either
22. holy/sacred
23. brave
24. little
25. happy

Q.3.
1. any, some
2. much
3. many
4. a few
5. a little
6. a little
7. a few

VOCABULARY

8. some
9. some
10. a lot of, a few
11. a little
12. a lot of, a little
13. each
14. faithful
15. either

Q.4.
1. more, most
2. far, farthest
3. hotter, hottest
4. little, less
5. bad, worst
6. pretty prettiest
7. luckier, luckiest
8. dirtier, dirtiest
9. lovelier, loveliest
10. dry, driest
11. shallow, shallower
12. clever, cleverest
13. Nobler, Noblest
14. wider, widest
15. fitter, fittest
16. slimmer, slimmest
17. merrier, merriest
18. Busy, busiest
19. worse, worst
20. many, most
21. In, innermost
22. up, uppermost
23. out, other
24. later/latter, latest/last
25. greyer, greyest
26. more famous, most famous
27. honest, most honest
28. more expensive, most expensive
29. courageous, more courageous
30. more handsome, most handsome
31. faster, fastest
32. worse, worst
33. better, best
34. more careful, most careful
35. broad, broader
36. sadder, saddest
37. young, youngest
38. old, oldest
39. kinder, kindest
40. greater, greatest
41. closer, closest
42. fonder, fondest
43. lazier, laziest
44. finer, finest
45. big, biggest
46. cold, coldest
47. thick, thicker
48. wide, wider
49. thin, thinnest
50. Tinier, Tiniest

Q.5.
1. most honest- Superlative degree
2. good-Positive degree
3. grand-Positive degree
4. elder-Comparative degree
5. happiest- Superlative degree
6. heavier- Comparative degree
7. greater-Comparative degree
8. good-Positive degree

9. beautiful-Positive degree
10. beautiful-Positive degree **Verb :** A Verb is a word used for saying something about some person or thing. Or, A Verb is a word that states something about a person or a thing.

Look at these sentences :
1. Aditi laughs.
2. The dog is dead.
3. The boys are eating food.
4. Aditya goes to school.
5. The policeman arrested the thief.

The words- *'laughs'*, *'is'*, *'are'*, *'goes'* and *'arrested'* have been used in the sentences given above which are saying something about - Aditi, the dog, the boys, Aditya and the Policeman respectively. Therefore, These words are verbs.

A verb may tell us:
(i) What a person or thing does; as,
   1. Ramita sings.
   2. Boys run quickly.
(ii) What is done to a person or thing; as,
   1. The chair is broken.
   2. Binay is punished.
(iii) What a person or thing is; as,
   1. The dog is dead.
   2. Glass is brittle.

Kinds of verb

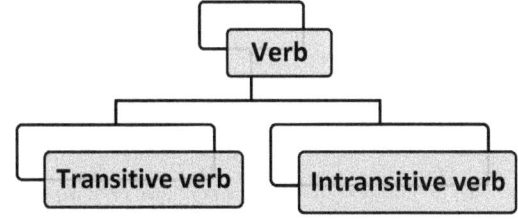

1. **Transitive and Intransitive verb**
   1. **Transitive verb :** A verb which required an object after it to complete its sense is called a Transitive verb; as,
      1. The man killed a snake.
      2. The boy opened the window.
      3. Aditi made a doll.

   In the sentences given above, The object - a snake, the window and a doll have been used after the verbs - killed, opened and made respectively which are clarifying the meaning of the used verbs- killed, opened and made. Therefore, these are Transitive verbs.

   2. **Intransitive verb :** A verb which does not require an object to complete its sense, but makes good sense by itself, is called an intransitive verb; as,
      1. Then man died
      2. The girl smiled
      3. The sun shines

   In the sentences given above, The verbs - died, smiled and *'shies'* have been used which are clarifying their meaning without objects. Therefore, These are Intransitive verbs.

Note : (i) When the Interrogative word - *'what'* or *'whom'* is used to ask a question from the sentence, we get something as an answer. That is an object and the verb is transitive.

Some Important facts of verb

Rule (1) : Some transitive verbs such as - give, ask offer, promise, tell, ... etc take two objects- an indirect object and a direct object. Person expressing words are called Indirect object and thing expressing words are called direct object. The indirect object is used before the direct object or the direct object is used after the indirect object; as,

Subject	Verb	Indirect object	Direct object
1. She	gave	me	an apple.
2. The teacher	told	us	a story.
3. I	offered	him	some money.
4. He	promised	us	a holiday.
5. She	asked	me	its price.
6. Will you	make	me	a cup of tea?
7. Can you	get	me	a dozen eggs?

Note: Using the preposition - *'to'* or *'for'*, The direct object can be written before it (=the preposition - *'to'* or *'for'*) and The Indirect object can be written after it (= the preposition-*'to'* or *'for'*); as,

Subject	Verb	Direct object	Preposition	Indirect object
1. She	gave	an apple.	to	me
2. The teacher	told	a story.	to	us
3. I	offered	some money.	to	him
4. He	promised	a holiday.	to	us
5. She	asked	its price.	to	me
6. Will you	make	a cup of tea?	for	me
7. Can you	get	a dozen eggs?	for	me

Rule(2) : Some verbs are used in the transitive verb form or in the Intransitive verb form without any change of form; as,

	Transitive		Intransitive
1.	I walk my horse everyday	1.	The horse walks.
2.	The horse drew the cart	2.	She drew near me.
3.	The driver Stopped the train	3.	The train stopped suddenly.
4.	The peon rang the bell.	4.	The bell rang.
5.	He moves the table	5.	The earth moves.

Note : The verbs - Come, go, fall, die, sleep, lie ..... etc. are used as Intransitive verbs.

Rule (3) : When an Intransitive verb is used with a preposition, it is formed Transitive verb (= it functions as a transitive verb); as,

1. He laughed at me.
2. She looked into the matter.
3. No one relies on my word.
4. I carried out his orders.
5. We take about the affair.

Note: Sometimes the preposition is used before the verb; as,

1. The Ganga river overflows its bank.
2. Akbar overcame the enemy.
3. He bravely withstood the attack.

Rule (4) : Somethings an object is used after the intransitive verb which is similar in meaning to the verb. Such an object is called cognate object Accusative.

Cognate object : An object similar in meaning to the verb is called a cognate object; as,

1. He died a glorious death.
2. He has fought a good fight.
3. She dreamt a strange dream.
4. She sang a sweet song.
5. He lived a virtuous life.

Rule (5) : Some Transitive verbs are sometimes used as Intransitive verbs; as,

	Transitive		Intransitive
1.	She eats bread.	1.	We eat to live.
2.	The boy broke the glass.	2.	The glass broke.
3.	He opened the door.	3.	The door soon opened.
4.	He burnt his fingers.	4.	He burnt with rage.
5.	The wind shook the house.	5.	The earth shook.

Rule (6) : When a noun modifies a verb, an adjective and an adverb and denotes time, place, distance, weight, value etc. it is called an adverbial object or adverbial accusative. It is in objective case or accusative case; as,

1. He went home.
2. The mobile set costs two thousand rupees.
3. He held the post for five years.
4. He can's wait a moment longer.
5. She swam a mile.

ENGLISH

Q.1. Pick out the verbs in the following sentences and say whether they are Transitive or Intransitive Verbs:

1. Aditya broke the slate.
2. He flies his kite.
3. Aditi received a prize.
4. He met a little cottage girl.
5. His wife spoke loudly.
6. The boy killed a snake.
7. He ran away quickly.
8. The policeman arrested the robber.
9. The children were playing.
10. I drink tea three times in a day.
11. Cocks crow in the morning.
12. It is very hot today.
13. She lives on fruit.
14. The Congress made Lal Bahadur Shastri Prime Minister.
15. His servant fells the three with an axe.
16. He saw her yesterday.
17. It has been raining all day.
18. The sun shines brightly.
19. The girl cut her finger with a knife.
20. The sun rises in the east.

Q.1 Pick out the objects in the following sentences and say whether they are Direct or Indirect objects.

1. The principal forgave him his faults.
2. He gave me an orange.
3. You gave her a twenty rupee note.
4. My grandmother told me a story.
5. Mr. Thakur taught them English.
6. He lent me five hundred rupees.
7. We gave him a prize.
8. The teacher asked him a question.
9. She told her husband a secret.
10. I promised to give him a TV set.
11. The guide shows us the way.
12. Pt. Teja Babu taught me Sanskrit.
13. Will you make a cup of coffee?
14. I taught the students a new lesson.
15. Kindly give me a pen.
16. Show me your fingers.
17. He brought me a glass of water.
18. He brought me some books.
19. I gave her a necklace.
20. Will you buy me some apples?

Q.3 Find out the error part of the following sentences:

1. The cricketers did not came out victorious, (1)/yet they were not disappointed (2)/ rather satisfied because (3) / they had played well. (4) / No error (5)

2. He complained to the police (1)/that his briefcase had been stolen (2)/ and that was lifted (3) / without any money. (4) / No error (5)

3. Can I (1) / lend your book (2)/ for an hour, please ? (3)./No error (4)

4. The manager called the clerk and said whether (1)/he was in the habit of (2) / sleeping at home as well (3)./ No error (4)

5. The telescope (1) / was discovered (2) by Galileo. (3)/No error (4)

6. The book on Political Science (1)/ brought in the market recently (2)/ is really an asset (3) / for all college students. (4) / No error (5)

7. While going (1)/ through to report (2)/ yesterday I founded (3) /several factual mistakes. (4) / No error (5)

8. The eminent speaker's speech (1)/ was broadcasted over (2)/ all the major radio stations. (3) / No error (4)

9. The terrorist (1)/ will certainly be hung (2)/ because the charges brought upon (3) / him are very serious. (4) / No error (5)

10. Hardly had he went (1)/ out of the class (2)/ when a mob of angry students (3) /attacked him. (4) / No error (5)

11. The Chief Minister said that his party would not repeat the mistakes (2)/ done by the (3) / previous government. (4) / No error (5)

12. Mr. Mehta is very (1)/ drunk so (2)/ he cannot tell (3) /me even his father's name. (4) / No error (5)

13. If I knew (1)/that my friend had to visit the town today, (2)/ I would have make his stay comfortable. (3) / No error (4)

14. He laid unconscious for half an hour (1)/ until he was seen (2)/ by a passing motorist. (3) /No error (4)

15. You must (1)/ not held in high esteem (2)/ those who are (3) / dangers to our society. (4) / No error (5)

ANSWERS WITH EXPLANATION

Q.1
1. broke - T. verb
2. flies - T. verb
3. received - T. verb
4. met - Int. verb
5. spoke - Int. verb
6. killed - T. verb
7. ran away - Int. verb
8. arrested - T. verb
9. were playing - Int. verb
10. drink - T. verb
11. crow - Int. verb
12. is - Int. verb
13. lives - Int. verb
14. made - T. verb
15. fells - T. verb
16. saw - T. verb
17. has been raining - Int. verb
18. shines - Int. verb
19. cut - T. verb
20. rises - Int. verb

Note: (i) T. verb : Transitive verb
(ii) Int. verb : Intransitive verb

Q.2.
1. him - Ind. object
   his faults - D. object
2. me - Ind. object
   an orangs - D. object
3. Her - Ind. object
   a twenty rupee note - D. object
4. me - Ind. object
   a story - D. object
5. them - Ind. object
   English - D. object
6. me - Ind. object
   five hundred rupees - D. object
7. him - Ind. object
   a prize - D. object
8. him - Ind. object
   a question - D. object
9. her husband a secret - D. object
10. him - Ind. object
    a TV set - D. object
11. us - Ind. object
    the way - D. object
12. me - Ind. object
    Sanskrit - D. object
13. a cup of coffee - D. object
14. the students - D. object
    a new lesson - D. object
15. me - Ind. object
    a pen - D. object
16. me - Ind. object
    your fingers - D. object
17. me - Ind. object
    a glass of water - D. object
18. me - Ind. object
    some books - D. object
19. her - Ind. object
    a necklace - D. object
20. me - Ind. object
    some apples - D. object

Note: (i) D. object : Direct object
(ii) Ind. object : Indirect object

Q.3

1. (1) M.V^1 -come will be used in place of M.V^2 - came because M.V^1 is used after do/does/did but M.V^2 is not used after do/does/did.

2. (3) M.V^2 - left will be used in place of M.V^2 - lifted. 'Lift' means *'to raise somebody/ something or be raised to a higher position or level'* and its past participle or V^3 form is lifted. While (whereas) *'leave'* means 'to go away from a person or place' and its past participle of V^3 form - 'left' is suitable for the meaning of the given sentence.

3. (2) V^1 - form - *'borrow'* will be used in place of V^1 - form - 'lend' because the V^1 - form- *'borrow'* means *'to take and use something that belongs to somebody else, and return it to them at a later time'* while (whereas) the V^1 - form 'lend' means 'to give something to somebody or allow them to use something that belongs to you, which they have to return to you later'.

4. (1) The verb-asked will be used in place of the verb - said because that verb-*'asked'* is used before *'whether'*.

5. (2) The verb - 'invented' will be used in place of the verb- 'discovered' because the verb - Invent means 'to produce or design something that has not existed before' and the verb-discover means-'to be the first person to become aware that a particular place or thing exists'. So, the verb-'invented' is suitable for the meaning of the given sentence.

Note: (i) Discover means tracing out something pre-existing but unknown

(ii) Invent means finding out something new.

6. (2) The verb-*'Introduced'* will be used in place of the verb- 'brought' because the V^1 - form - 'bring' means-'to come to a place with somebody/something' and its past form is -'brought' while (whereas) the V^1 - form - 'Introduce' means 'to make something available for use, discussion etc. for the first time' (or bring in) and its past form is introduced. So, the verb- 'introduced' is suitable for the meaning of the given sentence.

7. (3) The verb - 'found' will be used in place of the verb- 'founded' - because the verb - 'find' means- 'to discover somebody/something unexpectedly or by chance' and its past form is 'found' while (whereas) the verb found means-'to start something, such an organization or an institution especially by providing money' and its past form is 'founded'. Therefore, The verb-'found' is suitable for the meaning of the given sentence.

8. (2) The verb-'broadcast' will be used in place of the verb-'broadcasted' because the present, past and past participle form of 'broadcast' is broadcast but not - 'broadcasted'. See oxford Advance Learner's Dictionary.

9. (2) The verb- 'hanged' will be used in place of the verb-'hung' because the V^1 form- 'hang' means 'to attach something or to be attached, at the top so that the lower part is free or the V^1 form - 'hang' means - 'to kill somebody, usually as a punishment, by tying a rope around the neck and allowing them to drop' and its past participle form - is 'hanged'. The past participle form - 'hanged' is suitable for the meaning of the given sentence.

ENGLISH

10. (1) The verb-'gone' will be used in place of the verb - 'went' because the past participle form or M. V^3 is used after 'had'.

11. (3) The verb - 'made' will be used in place of the verb -'done' because the phrase - 'make a mistake' means-an action or an opinion that is not correct, or that produces a result that you did not want and its passive form is 'A mistake made'. Therefore, the verb - 'made' is suitable for the meaning of the given sentence.

Remember :

Active	Passive
1. Make a mistake	A mistake made
2. Make a noise	A noise made
3. Score a goal	A goal scored
4. Commit a sin/crime	A sin/ crime committed

12. (2) The adjective - 'drunken' will be used in the place of the past participle form - 'drunk' because the past participle form of 'drink' is 'drunk' and 'drunken'. 'Drunk' is used as V^3 - form or past participle and 'drunken' is used past participle form as an adjective. Therefore, 'drunken' is suitable for the meaning of the given sentence.

13. (3) The verb-'made' will be used in place of the verb - 'make' because the past participle or $M.V^3$ is used after - 'would have'.

14. (1) The verb - lay will be used in place of the verb - 'laid' because the verb- lie means ' to be or remain in a flat position on a surface' and its past form is 'lay' while (where as) The verb-'lay' means 'to put somebody/something in a particular position, especially it is done gently or carefull'; 'to produce eggs' and its past form is laid. Therefore, the past form of - 'lie' - 'lay' is suitable for the meaning of the given sentence.

15. (2) The V^1 - form - 'hold' will be used in place of the V^2 - form - 'held' because the V^1 - form is used after the Modal Auxiliary Verb. So, the V^1 - form - 'hold' will be used after the Modal Auxiliary Verb -'must' but not the V^2/V^3-form.

ADVERBS

Adverb : An adverb qualifies a verb, an adjective or another adverb.

An adverb is also used to qualify a preposition, a conjunction, a noun, a pronoun and a sentence besides a verb, an adjective and an adverb.

as, He walks slowly.
You run fast.

In the sentences given above, The words - 'slowly' and 'fast' are qualifying the verbs - 'walks' and 'runs' respectively. Therefore, The words - 'Slowly and fast' are adverbs.

1. He is very good.
2. She is extremely beautiful.

In the sentences given above, The words - 'very' and 'extremely' are qualifying the adjectives- ' good and 'beautiful' respectively. Therefore, the words-'very and extremely' are adverbs.

1. I write very carefully.
2. The horse runs very fast.

In the sentences given above, The words - 'Very' is qualifying the adverbs - 'carefully and fast' respectively Therefore, the word -'very' is an adverb.

1. The kite flew exactly over my head.
2. She parked her car just at the gate.

In the sentences given above, The words – 'exactly and *just*' are qualifying the prepositions - 'over and at' respectively, Therefore, the words- 'exactly and just' are adverbs.

He hates her simply because she drinks whisky.
Mr. Karna reached the station a little before the train left for.

In the sentences given above, The words- 'Simply' and a 'little' are qualifying the conjunctions - 'because' and 'before' respectively, Therefore, the words- 'Simply' and a 'little' are adverbs.

e.ge Fortunately, the terrorist was caught.
Naturally, Tendulkar played well.

In the sentences given above, The words - 'Fortunately and naturally' are qualifying the sentences - ' The terrorist was caught' and 'Tendulkar played well' respectively. Therefore, the words- ' fortunately and naturally' are adverbs.

1. Only Veena can do this work.
2. Even she comes late.
3. At least you should come here.

In the sentences given above, The words - 'only', 'even' and 'at least' are qualifying the noun-'Veena', the pronouns -'she' and 'you' respectively. Therefore, the words- 'only', 'even' and 'at least' are adverbs.

Note: Only, 'even' and 'at least' are such adverbs which qualify a noun and a pronoun. But generally an adjective qualifies a noun and a pronoun.

Kinds of Adverb

1. Adverbs of Time
2. Adverbs of Place
3. Adverbs of Number/Frequency
4. Adverbs of Quantity/rang/extent/degree
5. Adverbs of Manner
6. Adverbs of Reason
7. Adverbs of Affirmation or Negation

1. **Adverbs of time :** The adverbs which express time are called Adverbs of time; such as,
Today, tomorrow, yesterday, last night, last day, last week, last month, last year, next day, next week, next month, next year, late, lately, now, just now, just, ago, daily, already, early, soon, the day after tomorrow, the day before yesterday, at present, presently, shortly, recently, immediately, instantly, before, since.....etc.

Look at these sentences :

1. He saw me yesterday.

2. I have seen her before.

In the sentences given above, The words - Yesterday, before, daily, soon and late have been used as adverbs to qualify the verbs - saw, seen, comes, return and arrived respectively which denote (express) time. Therefore, these are adverbs of time.

2. **Adverbs of Place** : The adverbs which express place are called adverbs of place. Such as - here, there hither, thither, up, within, in, out, away, down, everywhere, somewhere, nowhere, anywhere, without, above below, far, near, backward, inside, outside, outdoors, indoors, ... etc.

1. He was sitting here.
2. Mr. Thakur lived there.
3. My brother-in-law is out.
4. There is air everywhere.

In the sentences given above, the words - here, there, out, everywhere, above, below, up, away and backward have been used to qualify the verbs - sitting, lived, is, is, looks, looked, galloped and walk respectively which denote (express) place - Therefore, these are adverbs of place.

Note: Generally the words - above, below, up, down, within, without and in are used as prepositions; as,

1. Come in
2. He lives in this apartment.

In example (1) the word - 'in' has been used as an adverb.

In example (2), the word- 'in' has been used as a preposition.

3. **Adverbs of Number** : The adverbs which express the frequency or number of 'to be an action' are called Adverbs of numbers. Such as-

once, twice, thrice, again, seldom, always, never, often, securely, hardly, rarely, frequently, firstly, secondly, thirdly... etc.

Look at these sentences:
1. He has not seen her once.
2. The postman called again.
3. She seldom dances.
4. We always try to do our best.

In the sentences given above, the words - once, again, seldom, always, often and frequently have been used as adverbs to qualify the verbs - seen, called, dances, try, makes and comes respectively which denote (=express) number of frequency. Therefore, these are adverbs of number or frequency.

4. **Adverbs of Quantity** : The adverbs which express the quantity, area or extent of an adjective or an adverb are called Adverbs of quantity. Such as-

Too, very, quite, enough, rather, fairly, entirely, altogether, almost, partly, nearly, fully, so, well, wholly, partially, far....etc.

Look at these sentences:
1. He was to careless.
2. She was very tired.
3. His grandfather is entirely deaf.
4. He is rather busy.

In the sentences given above, the words - too, very, entirely, rather, fully, altogether, partly, nearly, almost and quite have been used as adverbs to qualify the adjectives - careless, tired, deaf, busy, prepared, mistaken, right, exhausted, ripe and wrong respectively which denote (=express) quantity. Therefore, these are adverbs of quantity.

5. **Adverbs of Manner** : The adverbs which express the method of 'to be an action' are called Adverbs of manner; such as,

Fast, hard, slowly, bravely, foolishly, wisely, loudly, soundly, badly, carefully, fluently, beautifully, clearly, lovingly, faithfully, seriously, so, agreeably, certainly, well doubtfully, firm, conveniently, ..etc.

Note: Generally Adverbs of manner end with 'ly'.

VOCABULARY

Look at these sentences :
1. The horse ran fast.
2. He works hard.
3. Mr. Thakur walks slowly.

In The sentences given above, The words - fast, hard, slowly, bravely, foolishly, wisely, loudly, soundly, well and so have been used as adverbs to qualify the verbs - ran, works, walks, fought, behaved, acted, laughs, sleeps, written and do respectively which denote (=express) the method of 'to be an action'. Therefore, these are adverbs of manner.

6. **Adverbs of Reason :** The adverbs which express the sense of reason are called Adverbs of Reason; such as,
   Hence, therefore, consequently.

Look at these sentences:
1. Rambabu Thakur was hence unable to refund the charge.
2. She was therefore fined.
3. I therefore left school.

In the sentences given above, The words - hence, therefore and consequently have been used as adverbs to qualify the words - unable, fined, left and she respectively which denote (=express) the sense of Reason. Therefore, these are adverbs of reason.

7. **Adverbs of Affirmation or Negation :** The adverbs which express the sense of affirmation or negation are called Adverbs of Affirmation or Negation; such as,
   Not, surely, certainly, indeed, by no means, not at all, yes, no probably etc.

Look at these sentences:
1. She did not come after all.
2. Surely he is right.
3. She is certainly alive.
4. I do not know her.
5. Probably he will go.

Note: Sometimes two adverbs are used by adding a conjunction-'and' ; as,

Adverb + and + Adverb	Meanings
Again and again	more than once, repeatedly
By and by	before long, presently, after a time
Far and near	in all directions
Far and wide	Comprehensively
Far and away	by a great deal, decidedly, beyond all comparison
First and foremost	First of all
Now and then	from time to time, occasionally
Now and again	at intervals, sometimes, occasionally
Off and on	not regularly, intermittently
Once and again	on more than one occasion, repeatedly
Out and away	beyond comparison, by far
Out and out	decidedly, beyond all comparison
Over and above	in addition to, besides, as well as
Over and over	many times, frequently, repeatedly
Through and throught	thoroughly, completely
Thus and thus	in such and such away
To and fro	up and down, backwards and forwards

PRACTICE SET

Q.1 Pick out the Adverbs and state their Kinds:
1. An idle man is never happy.
2. Veena has lately returned form Mumbai.
3. She sings beautifully.
4. He often comes here.
5. He always tries to do his best.
6. The girl works hard.
7. These bananas are almost ripe.
8. He certainly went.
9. Lata sings delightfully.
10. The weather is delightfully cool.
11. Aditya slept soundly.
12. She seldom comes here.
13. Her father is out.
14. The sea is very stormy.
15. Don't go far.
16. He is far better now.
17. He is poor, hence he cannot pay fees.
18. When do you get up?
19. I don't know the time when she awakes.
20. How does he pay his fee?
21. This is the place where I live.
22. He is good enough for my purpose.
23. It is healthy to rise early.
24. The little children ran hither and hither.
25. There is air everywhere.
26. He spoke very angrily.
27. She sometimes comes here.
28. Once or twice I met her there.
29. Today, My son got up very early.
30. She is going to Gaya shortly.

Q.2 Fill the blanks with suitable forms of Adverbs given in the brackets:
1. She works........ . (hard/hardly)
2. My brother .... does any work. (hard/hardly)
3. He writes .... (clean/cleanly)
4. I have not seen her........ . (late/lately)
5. Chintoo and Pintoo are.... related (near/nearly)
6. His girl friend was .... dressed. (pretty/prettily)
7. He arrived....... . (late/lately)
8. Stand....... . (nearly/near)
9. One should fix one's hopes .... (highly/high)
10. The story of this film is .... amusing. (highly/high)

Q.3 Correct the following sentences:
1. He is too glad to meet you.
2. Peace is too kind for man.
3. It is very hot to play cricket.
4. The rabbit runs enough fast to win the race.
5. Aditya has acted enough boldly to deserve praise.
6. When his dearest wife died, he was little sorry.
7. When Aman felt little hungry and thirsty, he cried for help.
8. He is very more intelligent than Rahul.
9. Krish is much very stronger Ashish.
10. He is very the best player in his cricket team.
11. You talk very but do nothing.
12. He is very obliged to you.

13. That news was much distressing.
14. This sum is much difficult but that is much easy.
15. He is very interested in your story.
16. It gives much too pain.
17. It is too much painful.
18. My sister-in-law will be to only glad to see me.
19. He is present a teacher.
20. Rahul wants to stand first in the Board Examination and so he works hardly.

Q.4 Find out the error part of the following sentences:

1. I came directly (1)/ to my residence (2)/ from the airport. (3) / No error (4)
2. She does not hardly (1)/ know what (2)/ happened yesterday. (3) / No error (4)
3. I was most (1)/ unfortunate that he (2)/ died at the (3) / early age of 41. (4) /No error (5)
4. In the last week (1)/ I told him to come (2)/ in time but he still (3) / comes late every day. (4)/ No error (5)
5. The real important thing (1)/ of our life is our livelihood (2)/which discriminates us from animals. (4)/ No error (5)
6. She is too much beautiful (1)/ so most of the boys (2)/ run after her and (3) / want to influence her. (4) No error (5)
7. Whenever is the matter (1)/ I shall do this work (2)/ because I have to expose (3) / my working capacity at any cost. (4)/ No error (5)
8. The culprits of (1)/ the bomb explosion have (2)/ not yet (3) /been discovered. (4) / No error (5)
9. Whatever work (1)/ that which you undertake (2)/ put your best (3) / efforts in it. 4) / No error (5)
10. Your scooter would not (1)/ have given you so much trouble (2)/ if you had (3) / maintained it proper. (4) / No error (5)
11. The taxi driver who had come (1)/ to receive us at (2)/ the airport was speaking (3) / fluently French. (4) / No error (5)
12. Whenever you speak (1)/ take care that (2)/ others are not hurt (3) / by your words (4) / No error (5)
13. I (1)/ was delighted (2)/ to see him (3) / fully recover. (4) / No error (5)
14. The observers feel that (1)/ the stronger team has to face defeat (2)/ because that players (3) / don't play whole hearted. (4) / No error (5)
15. Although he is usually (1)/ rude with everyone (2)/ he behaved nice with (3) / all of us today. (4) / No error (5)
16. He ran so fastly (1)/ that he reached (2)/ the destination in (3)/ just two minutes. (4)/ No error (5)
17. In spite of toiling (1)/very hardly he (2) / realized that he had (3)/ not earned anything substantial. (4)/No error (5)
18. We were very much (1)/ carefully in our approach (2)/ and hence we would (3)/complete the complicated task. (4)/No error (5)
19. Hard had he (1)//thrown the ball (2)/when it fell (3)/ on the ground. (4)/ No error (5)
20. We are confident (1) / enough to earn (2) / our livelihood by (3)/ toiling hardly. (4) / No error (5)

ENGLISH

ANSWERS WITH EXPLANATION

Q.1.

1.	never	:	Adverb of frequency/number
2.	lately	:	Adverb of time
3.	Beautifully	:	Adverb of manner
4.	often	:	Adverb of frequency/number
	here	:	Adverb of place
5.	always	:	Adverb of frequency
6.	hard	:	Adverb of manner
7.	almost	:	Adverb of degree or quantity
8.	certainly	:	Adverb of affirmation
9.	delightfully	:	Adverb of manner
10.	delightfully	:	Adverb of degree or quantity
11.	soundly	:	Adverb of manner
12.	seldom	:	Adverb of frequency
	here	:	Adverb of place
13.	out	:	Adverb of place
14.	very	:	Adverb of degree or quantity
15.	far	:	Adverb of place
16.	far	:	Adverb of degree or quantity
17.	hence	:	Adverb of Reason
18.	when	:	Interrogative Adverb of time
19.	when	:	Relative Adverb
20.	how	:	Interrogative Adverb of manner
21.	where	:	Relative Adverb
22.	enough	:	Adverb of degree or quantity
23.	early	:	Adverb of time
24.	hither	:	Adverb of place
	thither		
25.	everywhere	:	Adverb of place
26.	very	:	Adverb of degree or quantity
	angrily	:	Adverb of manner
27.	sometimes	:	Adverb of frequency
	here	:	Adverb of place
28.	once	:	Adverb of frequency
	twice		
	there	:	Adverb of place
29.	today	:	Adverb of time
	very	:	Adverb of degree
	early	:	Adverb of time
30.	shortly	:	Adverb of time

Q.2.

1. hard 2. hardly
3. cleanly 4. lately
5. nearly 6. prettily
7. late 8. near
9. high 10. highly

Q.3

1. He is very glad to meet you.
2. Peace is very kind for man.
3. It is too hot to play cricket.
4. The rabbit runs fast enough to win the race.
5. Aditya has acted boldly enough to deserve praise.
6. When his dearest wife died, he was a little sorry.
7. When Aman felt a little hungry and thirsty, he cried for help.
8. He is much more intelligent than Rahul.
9. Krish is very much stronger than Ashish.
10. He is the very best player in his cricket team.
11. You talk much but do nothing.
12. He is much obliged to you.
13. That news was very distressing.
14. This sum is very difficult but that is very easy.

VOCABULARY

15. He is much interested in your story.
16. It gives too much pain.
17. It is much too painful
18. My sister-in-law will be only too glad to see me.
19. He is presently a teacher.
20. Rahul wants to stand first in the Board Examination and so he works hard.

Q.4

1. (1) *'Went straight'* will be used in place of 'came directly' in the given sentences.

2. (1) The negative word-'not' will not be used before the adverb - 'hardly' because the adverb- 'hardly' itself has a negative meaning.

3. (4) The adverb - 'early' will not be used in the given sentence because the phrase - 'at the age of 41' itself denotes 'early age'. Therefore, the adverb - 'early' is not suitable for the given sentence and also unnecessary for the meaning of the given sentence.

4. (1) 'In the' will not be used in the given sentence. Because 'In the' is not used before 'last + week /month/year'.

5. (1) The word - 'really' will be used in place of the word - 'real' because the word - 'real' is an adjective and the word - 'really' is an adverb. The word - 'important' is an adjective. An adverb is always used to qualify an adjective but an adjective is not used to qualify an adverb. Therefore, The adverb - 'really' will be used to qualify the adjective -'important' in the given sentence; as,
   A really important thing (√)
   A real important thing (x)

6. (1) The word-'very' will be used in place of the word - 'Too much' because The word - 'Too much' is used in the sense of 'very much' before a noun in negative sense. But the Adverb - 'very' is used in the sense of 'much' (=Bahut) before an adjective or an adverb.

   In the first part (1) of the given sentence, The adjective-'beautiful' has been used. Therefore, An adverb can be used to qualify it; as,
   She is very beautiful. (√)
   I run very fast. (√)

7. (1) 'Whatever the matter is' will be used in place of 'whenever is the matter'. Because 'whenever' is used 'at anytime that' ; 'on any occasion that' to denote time. But 'whatever' is used in the sense of 'any or every'; 'anything or everything' to denote a thing. Whenever/ Whatever/ Whichever/ Wherever + Subject + Verb is used in a sentence. But Whenever/ Whatever/ Whichever/Wherever + Verb + Subject is not used in a sentence; as,
   Wherever she had a cold, she ate only fruit. (√)
   I'll do whatever you want. (√)

8. (3) The word - 'yet' will not be used in the third (3) part of the given sentence - because the adverb - 'yet' is used in the sense of 'to talk about something that has not happened but that you expect to happen or until the time of speaking' in the last of negative sentences of Present Perfect Tense. Therefore, The adverb-'yet' will be used in the fourth (4) part of the given sentence.

9. (2) 'That which' will not be used because 'whatever' is used in the sense of 'of any sort degree as an adjective adn 'That', 'which' or 'that which' is not used after it (whatever). 'Whatever + noun+ subject + verb' is used in a sentence.

10. (4) The word - 'properly' will be used in place of the word - 'proper' because' subject + verb + object + adverb' is used in a sentence. In the given sentence, the object - 'it' has been used after the verb - 'maintained'. Therefore, The adverb - 'properly' will be used after the object - 'it' but the adjective - 'proper' will not be used after the object - 'it'.

ENGLISH

11. (4) *French fluently* will be used in place of 'fluently french' because 'Subject + verb + object + adverb of manner' is used in a sentence.

Remember :

(i) 'Subject + Adverb of manner + verb + object' is used in a sentence; as, She fluently speaks English. (✓)

But 'Subject + verb + Adverb of manner + object' is not used in a sentence; as, She speaks fluently English. (x)

12. (5) Given sentence is correct.

13. (4) 'Fully recovered' will be used in place of 'fully recover' in the given sentence. 'Fully recovered' is used before an adjective as an adverb of quantity but 'fully recovered' is not used before a verb. The word - 'recover' is a verb while (where as) the word - 'recovered' is the past participle form of the verb - 'recover'. The past participle - 'recovered' is also used as an adjective. Therefore, 'fully recovered' will be used in the given sentence but 'fully recover' will not be used in the given sentence.

14. (4) 'Heartedly' will be used in place of 'hearted'. Because 'hearted' is an adjective while 'heartedly' is an adverb. An adverb is used to qualify a verb but an adjective is not used to qualify a verb. Therefore, the adverb - 'heartedly' will be used to qualify the verb - 'play' in the given sentence. But the adjective - 'hearted' will not be used to qualify the verb - 'play' in the given sentence.

15. (3) 'Nicely' will be used in place of 'nice'. An adverb is used to qualify a verb but An adjective is not used to qualify a verb.

The word - 'nice' is an adjective while (where as) the word - 'nicely' is an adverb. Therefore, The adverb-'nicely' will be used to qualify the verb- 'behaved' in the given sentence. but the adjective - 'nice' will not be used to qualify the verb - 'behaved'. Generally An adjective is used to qualify a noun and a pronoun but An adjective is not used to qualify a verb; as,

It is a nice story. (✓)
It is a nicely story. (x)
She behaved nicely with me. (✓)
She behaved nice with me. (x)

16. (1) The word - 'fast' will be used in place of the word - 'fastly'. 'Fastly' is a slang word which is not used in English language, The word- 'Fast' is used as an adjective and an adverb; as,

Aditya is a <u>fast</u> <u>runner</u>. (✓)
Aditya is a fastly runner. (x)
He <u>runs</u> <u>fast</u>. (✓)
He runs fastly. (x)

17. (2) The word - 'hard' will be used in place of the word - 'hardly'. 'Hardly' is used in the sense of 'almost no' | 'almost not' | 'almost none'. While 'hard' is used in the sense of 'with great effort', 'with difficulty', 'with great force'. The adverb - 'hard' is suitable for the meaning of the given sentence.

18. (2) The word - 'careful' will be used in place of the word - 'carefully' because An adjective is used after the verb to be - is, are, am, was, were but an adverb is not used after the verb to be - is, are, am, was, were; as,

She <u>is</u> <u>careful</u> (✓)
She <u>is</u> <u>carefully</u>. (x)

19. (1) The word -'hardly' will be used in place of the word - 'hard'.

20. (4) The word - 'hard' will be used in place of the word-'hardly'.

PREPOSITION

Pre + position = Preposition

'*Pre*' means '*before*' while '*position*' means place.

Preposition : A preposition is a word used before a noun or pronoun to show its relation with the other words of the sentence; as,

1. The book is *on* the table.
2. The pen is *in* the inkpot.
3. The cat is *under* the table.
4. The book is *between* the inkpot and the chair.
5. The boy is *behind* the hut.

CORRECT USE OF PREPOSITIONS

(A) Use of 'At'

Rule (1) : '*At*' is used in the sense of '*in*' (Mai) Before the name of smaller places; as,

My brother lives at Jajur.

(=village)

I live at Musallahpur Hat.

(=Muhalla/colony)

Rule (2) : '*At*' is used to express the sense of 'destination' (=aim) after the following words; as,

Shout at	grumble at	shoot at kick aim at	laugh at smile at	mock at growl at	bite at
look at					

Rule (3) : '*At*' is used in the sense of 'on' or 'in' (Pr/Mai) to express time; as,

He will reach at 5 a.m.

He came at 6 o' clock.

Rule (4) : '*At*' is used before the following words; as

At home	At the station	At a party	At page 50
At school	At the	At a	At the
At college	At the airport	At a match	At a conference
At university	At the theatre	At a lecture	
At the bridge	At the bus stop	At a concert	
	At the platform	At the top	

Rule (5) : '*At*' is used before Time expressing words; as,

At night	At noon	At dawn	At dusk
At midnight	At afternoon	At daybreak	At twilight

Rule (6) : '*At*' is used before the following words; as,

At this moment   At bed time
At this juncture   At this hour
At Easter   At Christmas

Rule (7) : '*At*' is used before rate/price or speed expressing words; as,

Milk sells at Rs. 40/- a litre.

(=rate)

He got that book at Rs. 250.

(=price)

Rule (8) : '*At*' is used to express temporary action; as,

He is at work.

Means- He is working now.

She is at play.

Means- She is playing now.

Rule (9) '*At*' is used before 'age' and 'stage' expressing words; as,

My grandfather died at the age of sixty.

I left college at twenty five.

(B) Use of 'In'

Rule (1) : 'In' is used before the name of bigger places such as- country, continent, state, metropolises, city etc. as,

We live in India.

(=Country)

India is in Asia.

(=Continent)

She lived in Uttar Pradesh.

(=State)

Mr. Thakur lives in Patna.

(=City)

My father-in-law lives in Mumbai.

(=Metropolises)

Rule (2) : 'In' is used in the following phrases; as,

In the night   In the evening
In the morning   In the afternoon

ENGLISH

Rule (3) : '*In*' is used in the sense of '*in*' (Mail) or Inside of (Ke Andar) before the following words; as,

In the world	In a newspaper	In a queue	In a city
In the sky	In a street	In a village	In the house
In a letter	In the room	In hospital	In the bus
In a town	In the bag	In the rain	
In prison	In church		

Look at these sentences;

1. We live in the world.
2. He is in the room.
3. Twenty passengers were sitting in the bus.

Rule (4) : '*In*' is used to express permanent action; as,

His brother is in the Army.
He is in the Navy.
I am in the education.
He is in the politics.

Rule (6) : '*In*' is used before the phrasal structure-'A/An + *car/taxi/jeep* ; as,

He goes to college in a car. (√)
She went to school in a jeep. (√)
Her lover goes to the office in a taxi. (√)
He goes to college by a car. (×)
She went to school by a jeep. (×)
Her lover goes to the office by a taxi. (×)

(C) Use of '*Into*'

Rule (1) : '*Into*' is used to express the sense of - 'motion inside anything'; as,

The frog fell into the well.
He jumped into the river.
The robbers broke into my house.

Rule (2) : '*Into*' is used to show changing from one medium to another medium or one state/stage to another state/stage; as,

Translate into English.
Milk truns into curd.
Water turns into ice.

(D) Use of 'On'

Rule (1) : 'On' is used in the sense of 'at' (=Pr) to express the sense of 'place touching' (=Sthan Sparsh); as,

There are two books on the table.
He was carrying a suitcase on his head.
The headmaster is sitting on a wheel chair.

Rule (2) : 'On' is used in the sense of '*Ko*'/'*Pr*' before time expressing words to express the sense of 'certiainty'; as,

On Monday	On Tuesday
On Monday evening	On the morning of the event
On the same night	On the evening of the 1st January

* '*In*' is not used before the time expressing words given above; as,

In Monday	(×)
In Tuesday	(×)
In Monday evening	(×)
In the following evening	(×)
In the morning of the event	(×)
In the same night	(×)
In the evening of the 1st January	(×)

Rule (3) : 'On' is used before the phrasal structure -'A/An/the + bus/train/aeroplane/ship'; as,

He was on a bus/ a train/ a plane/ a ship.

Rule (4) : 'On' is used before the phrasal structure - 'A/An + cycle/scooter/ motorcycle'; as,

He was on a cycle / a scooter/ a motorcycle.

Rule (5): 'On' is used before 'Possessive Adjectives + cycle / scooter / motorcycle'; as,

Rule (6) " 'On' is used before the following words or phrases such as - foot, a horse, horse's back, a camel, camel's back, an elephant, elephant's back, a buffalo, buffalo's back, etc; as,

He walks on foot. He was riding on a horse.

Rule (7) : 'On' is used in the sense of 'towards' (=Ki or) to denote direction; as,

The robber drew a dagger on him.

(E) Use of 'Between'

Rule (1) : 'Between' is used in the sense of 'in the middle of' (=Ke Bich Mai) for two persons or things; as,

1. She was sitting between her husband and her father. (√)
2. Divide these mangoes between you and me. (√)
3. She was sitting between her husband to her father. (×)
4. Divide these mangoes between you and I. (×)

(F) Use of 'Among'

Rule (1): 'Among' is used in the sense of 'in the middle of' (=Ke Bich Mai) for more than two persons or things; as,

Divide thse mangoes among the children. (√)
Divide these mangoes between the children.(×)

(G) Use of 'Beside' and 'Besides'

❖ 'Beside' is used in the sense of 'by the side of' or 'out side', next to or at the side of somebody/ something; as,
Go and sit beside your father.
The child was sitting beside the mother.

❖ While 'Besides' is used in the sense of 'in addition to somebody/something'; a part form somebody/something; as,
Besides Shweta, all of the girls were present in the class.
Besides the Ramayana, I have read the Gita.
Besides Urdu, I know English and Hindi.

(H) Use of 'Above'

Rule (1) : 'Above' is used in the sense of 'at or to higher place or position than something/ somebody'; as,

The kites rose above the cloud.
The aeroplane is flying above the cloud.
The water came above our knees.
The people in the apartment above mine.

Rule (2) : 'Above' is used in the sense of '*more than something*' ; greater in number or quantity'; as,

There are above fifty students in the class.
(= There are more than fifty students in the class.) number
Her expenses are above her means.

(= Her expenses are more than her income.) quantity
Inflation is above 6%
Temperatures have been above average.

Rule (3) : 'Above' is used in the sense of 'superior to' ; 'too good or too honest to do something' ; as,

Sudhir ji is a publisher above suspicion.
(= Sudhir Ji is a completely trusted publisher.)

Rule (4) 'Above' is used in the sense of '*greater in level than something*' ; as,

Mount Everest is 8,850 metres above sea level.

Rule (5) : 'Above' is used in the sense of 'greater in age than somebody' ; as,

We can not accept children above the age of 10.

(I) Use of 'Over'

Rule (1) : 'Over' is used in the sense of 'resting on the surface of somebody/ something and party or completely covering them /it'; as,

Please spread the cloth over the table.
She put a blanket over the sleeping child.
He wore an overcoat over his suit.
She put her hand over her mouth to stop herself from screaming.

Rule (2) : 'Over' is used in the sense of '*In or to a position higher than but not touching somebody*/something'; as,

The clouds are over our heads.
The plane is flying over the town.
They held a large umbrella over her.
There was a lamp hanging over the table.

Rule (3) : 'Over' is used in the sense of '*to be over*' ; as,

The college is over at 4 p.m.
(= *The college ends at 4 p.m.*)

(J) Use of 'Upon'

'Upon' is used to express 'things in motion'; as,

The dog sprang upon the table.

The lion sprang upon the prey.

Note :

(i) 'Upon' is used in the sense of 'on'; as,

The decision was based upon two considerations.

(ii) 'Upon' is used to emphasize that three is a large number or amount of something; as,

Mile upon mile of dusty road.

Thousands upon thousands of letters.

(iii) 'Upon' is usually used in more formal contexts or in phrases such as

Once upon a time.

Row upon row of seats.

(iv) 'Almost upon you' is used in the sense of 'f something in the future is almost upon you, it is going to arrive or happen very soon'; as,

The summer season was almost upon them again.

(K) Use of 'Below'

Rule (1) : 'Below' is used in the sense of 'lower than'; as,

My father is below seventy. (√)

My father is under seventy. (×)

Rule (2) : 'Below' is used in the sense of 'lower than'; as,

His income is *below* Rs. 5000/- a month.(√)

His income is under Rs. 5000/- a month.(×)

Rule (3) : 'Below' is used in the sense of 'Inferior to'; as,

This work is *below* my dignity. (√)

This work is under my dignity. (×)

Note:(i) 'Below' is also used in the sense of 'at or to a lower level or position than somebody/ something'; as,

He dived below the surface of the water.

Please do not write below this line.

Skirts will be worn below (long enough to cover) the knee.

(L) Use of 'Under'

Rule (1) : 'Under' is used in the sense of 'in, to, or through a position that is below something'; as,

He was sitting under the tree.

The cat is sitting under the chair.

Have you looked under the bed?

She placed the ladder under (just lower than) the window.

The dog squeezed under the sense of '*under the power of*' (Adhin); as,

A writer is under the publisher.

Administration is under the government.

Rule (3) : 'Under' is used in the sense of '*less than*'; as,

She was under age.

(=*the age of her was less than proper/ requirement.*)

(M) Use of 'Beneath'

Beneath is used in the sense of 'in or to a lower position than somebody/something'; as,

He was sitting beneath the tree.

They found the body buried beneath a pile of leaves.

The boat sank beneath the waves.

But - 'Beneath' is also used in the sense of 'not good enough for somebody'; as,

He considers such jobs beneath him.

They thought she had married beneath her (=married a man of a lower social status)

Note : '*Both under an Beneath*' are used without any differences in the sense of 'in or to a lower position than somebody/ something'.

(N) Use of 'Behind'

Rule (1) : 'Behind' is used in the sense of 'at or towards the back of somebody/ something, and often hidden by it or them'; as,

My daughter was hiding behind the door.

He has left nothing behind him.

Don't forget to lock the door behind you (=when you leave).

The sun disappeared behind the clouds.

Rule (2) : 'Behind' is used in the sense of 'making less progress than somebody/ something' ; as, He is behind the rest of the class in reading.

We are behind schedule (=late.)

Rule (3) : 'Behind' is used in the sense of 'responsible for starting or developing something' ; as, What is behind that happy smile (=what is causing it)?

He was the man behind the plan to build a new hospital.

(O) Use of 'By'

Rule (1) : 'By' is used in the sense of 'near somebody/ something; at the side of somebody/ something; beside somebody/something'; In this sense, By and beside are used instead of 'each other' ; as,

The child came and sat by her.	(√)
The child came and sat *beside* her.	(√)
Her village is by the river.	(√)
He village is beside the river.	(√)

Rule (2) : 'By' is used in the sense of 'no later than the time mentioned' ; before the pointed out time; till; as,

The Rajdhani Express will arrive here by 11 o' clock.

By the end of this month, she will have returned from Mumbai.

He will have informed the police of the accident by tomorrow morning.

Rule (3) : 'By' is used in the sense of 'during something'; in a particular situation; as,

He travelled by night.	(√)
(=He travelled during night.)	
The sun shines by day.	(√)
(=The sun shines during day.)	
He travelled before night.	(×)
The sun shines before day.	(×)
We had to work by candle light.	(√)

Rule (4) : 'By' is used in the sense of 'Ke Dwara' before a passive object in passive voice; as,

The boy was beaten by the teacher.	(√)
The boy was beaten with the teacher.	(×)

Note: 'By' is usually used after a passive verb to show who or what does, creates or cause something; as,
1. He was knocked down by a bus.
2. I was frightened by the noise.

(P) Use of 'of'

Rule (1) : 'Of' is used in the sense of 'se' to express cause; as

She died of fever.
He died of malaria.
His wife is tired of work.
I am fond of music.

Note: (i) If a person dies because of 'illness' | 'disease', 'hunger' | 'starvation', 'thirst', 'grief' and 'shame', the preposition - 'of' is used after the verb - 'die'. But in this sense, the prepositions - from, with an dby are not used after the verb - 'die'; as,

Her died of grief.	(√)
He died from grief.	(×)

(ii) If a person dies because of 'wound', 'over eating', 'over drinking' and 'food poisoning', The preposition - 'From' is used after the verb - 'die'. But in this sense, the prepositions - of, with, by and for are not used after the verb - 'die'; as,

He died *from* a wound.	(√)
He died of a wound.	(×)

(Q) Use of 'Off'

Rule (1) : 'Off' is used in the sense of 'down or away from a place or at a distance in space or time' (at a distance from/ far from) to express separation; as,

There was a village a little way off the sea coast.
That old man fell of the ladder.
He put *off* his coat.

Rule (2) : 'Off' is used in the sense of 'leading away from something, for example a road or room'; as,

We live off Main street.
There is a bathroom off the main bathroom.

Rule (3) : 'Off' is used in the sense of 'away from work or duty'; as,
He has had ten days off school.
Rule (4) : 'Off' is used in the sense of 'away from a price'; as,
They knocked Rs. 5000/- off the car.
Rule (5) : 'Off' is used in the sense of 'not wanting or liking something that you usually eat or use'; as,

(R) Use of 'till and 'until'
'Till' or 'Until' is used in the sense of 'up to the point in time or the event mentioned' (Tak) before ending time while 'from' is used before starting time; as,
He works in the factory from 9 a.m. *till* 3 p.m.
He works in the factory from 9 a.m. *until* 3 p.m.
The street is full of traffic from morning till night.
He continued working up until his death.

(S) Use of 'In front of'
'In front of ' is used in the sense of 'in a position that is further forward than somebody/something but not very far away' (Ke Samne). It is generally used for things but it is also used to denote the position for a person;
There is a tree in front *of* my house. (√)
There was a beautiful garden in *front* of my school. (√)
There is a tree before my house. (×)
There was a beautiful garden before my school. (×)
The car in front of me stopped suddenly and I had to brake.
The bus stops right in front of our house.
He was standing in front of me in the line.
She spends all day sitting in front of (working at) her computer.

(T) Use of 'Around' and 'Round'
Rule (1) : 'Around' is used in the sense of 'surrounding somebody/something'; 'on each side of something', 'on to or from the other side of somebody/something' ; 'in a circle'; 'to fit in with particular people, ideas etc. ;in or to many places in an area'; 'here and there', and 'in different parts of'; as,
They were sitting around the garden.
Stop walking around and start some business.
Rule (2) : While 'Round' is used in the sense of 'surround' for circular path and curved path; as, We were sitting round the dinning table.
The earth moves round the sun.

(U) Use of 'Amid' and 'Amidst'
Rule (1) : 'Amid'/ 'Amidst' is used in the sense of 'In the middle of' to denote place; as,
A beautiful girl was sitting amid/amidst the young.
There was a small cottage amid/amidst the building.
Rule (2): 'Amid' | 'Amidst' is used in the sense of 'in the middle of' before uncountable nouns; But Among or Amongst is not used in this sense; as,
Honesty is useless amid/amidst dishonesty.

(V) Use of 'Up' and 'Down'
Rule (1) 'Up' is used in the sense of 'to or in a higher position somewhere', 'along or further, along a road or street', towards the place where a river starts; as a preposition; as,
She climbed up the fight of steps.
The village is further up the valley.
We live just up the road, past the post office.
A cruise up the Rhine.
Note: (i) 'Up' is used in the sense of 'towards or in a higher position', 'to or at a higher level', 'to the place where somebody/ something is' as an adverb; as,
   He got *up* to ask a question.
   Prices of articles are still going up.
   Stop writing, the time is up.
Rule (2) : 'Down' is used in the sense of 'from a high or higher point on something to a lower one', along, all through a period of time as a preposition; as,
The stone rolled down the hill.
Tears ran down her face.
Her hair hung down her back to her waist.
He lives just down the street.

VOCABULARY

(W) **Use of 'Through'**

Rule (1) : 'Through' is used in the sense of 'by means of'; as,

He knew it *though* a newspaper.

Rule (2) : 'Through' is used in the sense of 'from one end or side of something/ somebody to the other'; as,

The beggar went *through* the market.

Can you see *through* glass?

The burglar got in through the window.

The bullet went straight through him.

(X) **Use of 'Beyond'**

Rule (1) : 'Beyond' is used in the sense of 'the farther side of ; as,

Don't go *beyond* the river.

There is a village *beyond* the pond.

Rule (2) : 'Beyond' is used in the sense of 'later than a particular time' before the time expressing words; as,

Don't remain out beyond midnight.

(Y) **Use of 'During'**

Rule (1) : 'During' is used in the sense of 'in course of','all through a period of time'; as,

The sun given us light during the day.

Nobody would talk during my discourse.

Rule (2) : 'During' is used before 'certain period of time'; as,

During the war	During the winter
During the strike	During Easter
During the meeting	During his childhood/1947
During the middle age	During the function
During Deepawali	During the examination
During Holi	During the summer vacation
During the summer	
During the day	During the week
During the night	During the month
During the spring	During the year
	During the morning

Rule (3) : 'During' is used to express the sense of state; as,

The people suffer hardship during the war.

(Z) **Use of 'Against'**

Rule (1) : 'Against' is used in the sense of 'In contravention of (=opposing or disagreeing with somebody/something)' ; as,

The workers have acted *against* the orders of the director.

One should not go *against* the rule.

We are playing against the league champions next week.

She was forced to marry against her will

I'd advise you against doing that.

Rule (2) : 'Against' is used in the sense of 'opposite' ; as,

Sailing *against* the current is difficult.

It is difficult to paddle the cycle *against* the wind.

(A) **Use of 'Form'**

Rule (1) : 'From' is used in the sense of 'Se' to express separation (=to separate from a particular place) ; as,

He has come from Mumbai.

The wind blew from the South

The fruits have fallen from this tree.

Rule (2) : 'From' is used in the sense of 'Se' to express the sense of time before present, past or future time expressing words; as,

Mukesh will come here from Sunday next.

I attended the meeting from morning to evening.

He will teach the students from 10 a.m.

Rule (3) : 'From' is used in the sense of 'Se' to express the sense of cause; as,

His beloved has been suffering *from* fever.

(B) **Use of 'Across'**

Rule (1) : 'Across' is used in the sense of 'on the opposite side of'; as,

My elder sister lives across the Ganga river.

Rule (2) : 'Across' is used in the sense of 'from one side to the other' ; as,

There is a bridge *across* the river.

(C) **Use of 'About'**

Rule (1) : 'About' is used in the sense of 'on the subject of somebody/something'; as,

He has doubt about his honesty.

What do you know about this incident?

ENGLISH

Rule (2) : 'About' is used in the sense of 'approximately' ; as,
It is about eight o' clock.
The college is about six miles from my village.

(D) Use of 'Along'
Rule (1) : 'Along' is used in the sense of '*from one end to or towards the other end of something*' ; as,
They walked slowly along the road.
I looked along the shelves for the book I needed.
Rule (2) : 'Along' is used in the sense of '*In a line that follows the side of something long*' (=in the same line); as,
He was walking along the road.
Houses had been built along both sides of the river.

(E) Use of 'Before'
Rule (1) : - 'Before' is used in the sense of '*In the presence of who is listening or watching*' ; as a preposition; as,
She was standing before the police inspector.
The case was brought before the judge.
The accused appeared before the magistrate.
She said it before witness.
They had the advantage of playing before their home crowd.
Rule (2) : 'Before' is used in the sense of '*earlier than the time when* 'as a conjunction; as,
I take meal before going to my tuition centre.
The patient had died before the doctor came.
Did she leave a message before she went?
Rule (3) 'Before' is used in the sense of '*earlier than somebody/something*' as a preposition; as,
He arrived before me.
Leave your keys at reception before departure.

(F) Use of 'After'
Rule (1) : 'After' is used in the sense of '*later than something*'; '*following something in time*', before time expressing words as a preposition; as,
He went there *after* five days.
She went to her college *after* 11 a.m.
Tuesday comes *after* Monday.
April comes *after* March.
After winning the prize she became famous over night.
After an hour I went home (=when an hour had passed)
Rule (2) : 'After' is used in the sense of '*later than something*' before place expressing words as a preposition; as,
B comes *after* A.
From Patna, Hazipur comes after the Ganga river.
Rule (3) : 'After' is used in the sense of '*as a result of or because of something that has happened*' ; as,
I shall never forgive him after what he said.
Rule (4) : 'After' is used in the sense of '*despite something*' ; '*although something has happened*' ; as,
I can't believe she'd do that, not after all I've done for her.

(G) Use of 'With'
Rule (1) : 'With' is used in the sense of '*Se/Ke Dwara*' (using with) before an instrument or tool. With the help of which an action is done; as,
He writes with a pen.
She writes with a pencil.
He cuts the mango with a knife.
The carpenter cuts the tree with an exe.
But If the word - '*pencil*' is used as an uncountable noun; A is not used before it. The preposition - '*with*' is not used before it. Only the preposition - '*in*' is used before it; as,
He writes in pencil.   (√)
He writes in ink.   (√)
He writes with pencil.   (×)
He writes in a pencil.   (×)
Rule (2) : 'With' is used in the sense of '*In the company or presence of somebody/ something*'; as,
Subodh went to Shimla with his wife.
His son went to college with his friends.
A beautiful girl came with her lover.
Rule (3) : 'With' is used in the sense of '*in spite of*' or '*despite something*'; as,
With all his wealth, he is unhappy.
With all his bad habits, he is a good man.

Rule (4) : 'With' is used in the sense of 'Se' to express the sense of cause; as,
A young and beautiful girl was trembling with fear.
Your eyes are red with tears.

(H) Use of 'Without'

Rule (1) : 'Without' is used in the sense of 'because of something and as it happens'; as,
A woman cannot live without a man.
We cannot live without water.
One cannot write without a pen.
We cannot see without eyes.

Rule (2) : 'Without' is used in the sense of 'not having', 'experiencing' or 'showing something'; as,
They had gone two days without food.
He found the place without difficulty.
She spoke without much enthusiasm.

Rule (3) : 'Without' is used in the sense of 'not in the company of somebody'; as,
Don't go without me.

Rule (4) : 'Without' is used in the sense of 'not using or taking something'; as,
Can you see without your glasses?
Don't go out without your coat?

(I) Use of 'Within'

Rule (1) : 'Within' is used in the sense of 'Inside' before time and place expressing words; as,
I shall do it within an hour.
He will come within this month.
Patna Junction is within two kilometres from my residence.

Note : 'Within' is used in the sense of 'before the end of a period of time' while 'In' is used in the sense of 'at the end of a period of time',

Rule (2) : 'Within' is used in the sense of 'inside' to express the sense of capability and limitation; as,
We should keep our expenses within our income.
This is within a kilometre.

(J) Use of 'Towards'

Rule (1) : 'Towards' is generally used in the sense of 'In the direction of somebody/something'; as,
He was going towards the college.
She went towards office.
They were heading towards the German Border.
She had her back towards me.

Rule (2) : 'Towards' is used in the sense of 'per'; as,
My brother is kind towards the poor.

Rule (3) : 'Towards' is used in the sense of 'nearly'; as,
It is now towards night.

Rule (4) : 'Towards' is used in the sense of 'getting closer to achieving something'; as,
This is a first step towards political union.

(K) Use of 'To'

Rule (1) : 'To' is used in the sense of 'Towards something', 'In the direction of something' to show destination (=aim); as,
He was going to Patna Market.
She is going to Patna College.
I walked to the office.
He pointed to something on the opposite bank.

Rule (2) : 'To' is used in the sense of 'Till' before time or place expressing words; as,
She waited for me from morning to evening.
The postman delivers the letters from door to door.

Rule (3) : 'To' is used in the sense of 'before' to express the sense of 'time'; as,
It is quarter to ten.
(= It is fifteen minutes before ten o'clock.)
It is ten minutes to ten.
(= It is ten minutes before ten o'clock.)

Rule (4) : 'To' is used in the sense of 'on'; as,
He was invited to tea.
Her mother invited me to dinner.

Rule (5) : 'To' is used in the sense of 'Ke Prati' (per); as,
He must be careful to his duty.
Show affection to your neighbours.

ENGLISH

PRACTICE SET

Q.1. Fill in the blanks with suitable prepositions:

1. The calculator is .... the table.
2. He was angry ...... me.
3. That man is found guilty....theft.
4. Your teacher is not satisfied ...... your study.
5. He should take care.... his health.
6. Mukesh travelled ..... train.
7. She jumped...... the well
8. You must beware....... tigers.
9. He quarreled...... my brother.
10. The thieves broke...... his house.
11. R.K. Thakur is senior.....me.
12. Meena is satisfied......her husband.
13. His wife died......cancer.
14. My father was acquainted.....him.
15. He prefers tea......coffee.
16. I am fond......music.
17. My wife has been suffering.......fever for two days.
18. The teacher congratulated her.......her success.
19. Gandhi Ji was born.......1869.
20. The aeroplane was flying ....the clouds.

Q.2. Find out the error part of the following sentences:

1. They walked (1)/besides (2)/each other (3) / in silence. (4)/No error (5)
2. His relation (1) to Kalpana (2)/ is (3) / good. (4)/No error (5)
3. The teacher (1)/ has not (2)/control upon (3) / to reach there. (4)/No error (5)
4. We (1)/ travelled (2)/with steamer (3) / to reach there. (4)/ No error (5)
5. His statement (1)/ is very much (2)/similar about (3) / yours (4)/No error (5)
6. The shopkeeper (1)/ deals with grain (2)/but did not deal (3) / honestly with me. (4)/No error (5)
7. He (1)/ appealed to the judge (2)/ for his release (3) / from jail. (4)/No error (5)
8. I complained against (1)/ the magistrate (2)/against Munna (3) / about his misconduct. (4)/No error (5)
9. We (1)/ are (2)/ responsible for God (3) / for our actions. (4)/No error (5)
10. The doctor referred (1)/ the patient for the P.M.C.H. (2)/without (3) /examining him. (4)/No error (5)
11. My cousin has been (1)/ married with (2)/ the richest man (3) / of the village. (4)/ No error (5)
12. He was (1)/ shocked to hear that (2)/ her mother (3) / died of an accident. (4)/No error (5)
13. Mr. Kishori Thakur (1)/ is (2)/ blind (3) / with one eye. (4)/No error (5)
14. On a holiday (1)/ I prefer (2)/ writing than going out (3) / visiting friends. (4)/No error (5)
15. I have been working on (1)/ the problem from a long time (2)/ but is still not (3) / able to solve it. (4)/No error (5)
16. Mr. Mishra and his wife (1)/ were invited (2)/ for the cultural function (3) / at my house. (4)/ No error (5)
17. Beside chocolate (1)/ they also bought (2)/ many balloons (3) / for the child. (4)/No error (5)
18. Yesterday, Binay (1)/ came across with (2)/ one of his (3) / old friends (4)/No error (5)
19. Of what I know (1)/ of her (2)/ I hesitate to (3) / trust in him. (4)/No error (5)
20. He left to Delhi (1)/ this morning (2)/ for some (3) / official work. (4)/No error (5)

Q.3 Correct the following sentences:

1. His wife was dressed up black.
2. She is married with a rich man.
3. Are you careful to your health?
4. The old man died of overeating.
5. This is different to the other.

6. His suggestion was helpful for me.
7. Her dress is made up silk.
8. I depend over my publisher's word.
9. She is greedy of money.
10. He has no acquaintance to this man.
11. The publisher's capacity of hard work seems unlimited.
12. My wife prevented me to speaking.
13. What are you laughing?
14. Is Manu coming is plane?
15. Ruby has been absent from Monday last.
16. Mr. Thakur stood among Aditi and Aditya.
17. Poverty comes from idleness.
18. My brother-in-law travelled by a bicycle.
19. Did he stay on home yesterday?
20. The workers work in the factory from 10 a.m. and 4 p.m.

Q.4. Choose the most suitable preposition:

1. He was astonished .... the sad news.
   (a) at (b) in (c) with (d) to
2. He is confident .... his success.
   (a) of (b) for (c) about (d) towards
3. Exercise is beneficial .... health.
   (a) towards (b) for (c) to (d) in
4. My wife always grumbles .... her bad luck.
   (a) in (b) over (c) at (d) upon
5. We travelled .... boat to reach Sri Lanka.
   (a) by (b) on (c) for (d) about
6. His statement is very much similar .... mine.
   (a) to (b) of (c) about (d) on
7. He is jealous .... me.
   (a) with (b) into (c) of (d) at
8. She has a passion .... dance and music.
   (a) upon (b) at (c) in (d) for
9. He came .... me in the market.
   (a) at (b) into (c) across (d) of
10. No one can hinder him ....doing this.
    (a) into (b) from (c) for (d) of
11. Good sleep is necessary .... good health
    (a) of (b) for (c) at (d) from
12. I beg pardon........you for being late.
    (a) with (b) of (c) for (d) off
13. Only the blood stained road was a witness .... his assassination.
    (a) of (b) to (c) at (d) on
14. I continued to smile .... his threats.
    (a) at (b) on (c) upon (d) over
15. Fortune continued to smile......... me.
    (a) at (b) in (c) with (d) upon
16. Pakistan is supplying arms .... the terrorists.
    (a) with (b) for (c) to (d) against
17. America supplies Pakistan ....arms.
    (a) with (b) for (c) to (d) against
18. Contentment is essential ....happiness.
    (a) for (b) to (c) in (d) of
19. His house is adjacent .... mine.
    (a) with (b) to (c) from (d) of
20. She has strong antipathy ....smoking.
    (a) for (b) against (c) to (d) of
21. He is envious .... my achievements.
    (a) to (b) for (c) of (d) in
22. He stood .... the court charged with the murder of his wife.
    (a) in (b) for (c) before (d) of
23. Since he is ill, he is confined .... bed.
    (a) in (b) on (c) to (d) of
24. Some politicians are very sensitive .... criticism.
    (a) at (b) on (c) to (d) for
25. Shakespeare had a great insight .... human nature.
    (a) over (b) upon (c) for (d) into

ENGLISH

26. In the morning, Mr. Thakur simply takes a glance .... the newspaper headlines.
(a) at   (b) on   (c) of   (d) through

27. We must conform .... the rules of the game.
(a) in   (b) at   (c) from   (d) to

28. A honorary degree was conferred .... him.
(a) at   (b) upon   (c) for   (d) on

29. The mother was concerned .... the safety of her child.
(a) at   (b) about   (c) for   (d) with

30. When I heard of my grandmother's death, I burst .... tears.
(a) at   (b) upon   (c) for   (d) in

Q.5. Find out error part of the following sentences:

1. The aircraft was overloaded (1) / there was something wrong of the battery (2)/ and the engine was making a queer noise.(3)/No error (4)

2. I warned him (1) / for the danger (2) / he was going (3) / to face during the hiking. (4) / No error (5)

3. Ordinarily, when in difficulty (1) / Renuka prefers keeping her counsel (2) / than running about (3)/ taking advice. (4) No error (5)

4. Sheela advised to (1) / her child not to (2) / play with the ball (3) / on the road. (4) / No error (5)

5. Basu was trying to pass (1) / through the gap on (2) / the fence when he (3) / tore his shirt. (4) / No error (5)

6. I have been teaching in this school (1) / since several years (2) / but have never met (3) / such a hopeless class as this. (4) / No error (5)

7. It is easy to see that (1) / a lawyer's demeanor in court (2) / may be prejudicial against the interests of his client. (3) / No error (4)

8. The reason we have not been able to pay income tax (1) / is due to fact (2) / that we did not receive pay on time. (3) / No error (4)

9. The policemen fired all the (1) / students when (2) / they were attacked (3) / by some of them. (4) / No error (5)

10. He was not promoted (1) / to the rank of colonel (2) / till for a few (3) / months of his resignation. (4)/ No error (5)

11. All the players (1) / except Sam (2) / were present (3) / on the field. (4) / No error (5)

12. Despite of a good monsoon (1) / this year, the production (2) / of food grains in the (3) / country did not go up. (4) / No error (5)

13. Yesterday, while (1) / crossing the road (2) / he was (3) run out by a truck. (4) / No error (5)

14. The girl wrote an essay (1) / so well (2) / that her teacher was exceedingly (3) / pleased at her. (4)/ No error (5)

15. He tried (1) / to open the cane (2) / by a cane opener. (3) No error (4)

16. When the students reached late (1)/ the teacher objected their entering the class (2) / without his permission. (3) / No error (4)

17. The captain and his (1) / wife were invited (2) / for the cultural (3) / function at my home. (4) / No error (5)

18. The government decided to (1) / write of the debts (2) / of the farmers who were (3) / below the poverty line. (4) / No error (5)

19. Children visiting the (1) / park are amused (2) / by the monkeys (3) / play in the cages. (4) / No error (5)

20. The great actor was (1) / angry with the treatment (2) / during the party (3) / in Ashoka Hall. (4) / No error (5)

VOCABULARY

ANSWERS WITH EXPLANATION

Q.1.

1. on	2. with	3. of	4. with
5. of	6. by	7. into	8. of
9. with	10. into	11. to	12. with
13. of	14. with	15. to	16. of
17. from	18. on	19. in	20. above

Q.2.

1. **(2)** *'Beside'* will be used in place of *'Besides'*.
2. **(2)** *'With'* will be used in place of *'To'*.
3. **(3)** *'Over'* will be used in place of *'Upon'*.
4. **(3)** *'By'* will be used in place of *'With'*.
5. **(3)** *'To'* will be used in place of *'About'*.
6. **(2)** *'In'* will be used in place of *'With'*.
7. **(5)** Given sentence is correct.
8. **(1)** *'To'* will be used in place of *'against'*.
9. **(3)** *'To'* will be used in place of *'for'*.
10. **(2)** *'To'* will be used in place of *'for'*.
11. **(2)** *'To'* will be used in place of *'With'*.
12. **(4)** *'died by an accident'* will be used in place of *'accident'*.
13. **(4)** *'Of'* will be used in place of *'with'*.
14. **(3)** *'To'* will be used in place of *'than'*.
15. **(2)** *'For'* will be used in place of *'From'*.
16. **(3)** *'To'* will be used in place of *'for'*.
17. **(1)** *'Besides'* will be used in place of *'Beside'*.
18. **(2)** *'Came across'* will be used in place of *'Came across with'* the preposition - *'with'* is not used with the phrasal verb - *'Came across'*.
19. **(1)** *'From'* will be used in place of *'of'*.
20. **(1)** *'For'* will be used in place of *'To'*.

Q.3.

1. His wife was dressed in black.
2. She is married to a rich man.
3. Are you careful about your health?
4. The old man died from overeating.
5. This is different from the other.
6. His suggestion was helpful to me.
7. Her dress is made of silk.
8. I depend on my publisher's word.
9. She is greedy for money.
10. He has no acquaintance with this man.
11. The publisher's capacity for hard work seems unlimited.
12. My wife prevented me from speaking.
13. What are you laughing at?
14. Is Manu coming by plane?
15. Ruby has been absent since Monday last.
16. Mr. Thakur stood between Aditi and Aditya.
17. Poverty comes of idleness.
18. My brother-in-law travelled on a bicycle.
19. Did he stay at home yesterday?
20. The workers work in the factory from 10 am to 4 pm.

Q.4.

1. (a)	2. (a)	3. (c)	4. (c)
5. (a)	6. (a)	7. (c)	8. (d)
9. (c)	10. (b)	11. (b)	12. (b)
13. (b)	14. (a)	15. (a)	16. (c)
17. (a)	18. (b)	19. (b)	20. (c)
21. (c)	22. (c)	23. (c)	24. (c)
25. (d)	26. (a)	27. (d)	28. (d)
29. (b)	30. (c)		

Q.5.

1. **(2)** The preposition-*'with'* will be used in place of - *'of'*.
2. **(2)** The preposition-*'of'* will be used in place of - *'for'*. because *'warn somebody of something (warn him of the danger)'* means *'give somebody notice of something'; 'Inform somebody in advance of what may happen'* which is suitable for the meaning of the given sentence.

ENGLISH

Remember:

Phrases	Meaning	Sentences
Warn somebody of something	give somebody notice of something; Inform somebody in advance of what may happen	I tried to warn her, but she won't listen. The local papers warned us of a communal riot.
Warn somebody about/against somebody/something	put somebody on his guard against somebody/something	He warned us against pick pockets at the railway booking office. The police have warned shopkeepers about the forged bank notes.
Warn somebody off (something/ doing something)	give somebody notice that he must go or stay away e.g., from private property	I had been warned off visiting her while she was still unwell.

3. **(3)** The preposition-'*to*' will be used in place of '*than*'.
   Because the preposition - '*To*' is used after the verb- '*prefer*'.

4. **(1)** The preposition-'*to*' will not be used in the given sentence.
   Because the preposition - '*to*' is not used before the object of the verb-advise.

5. **(2)** The preposition-'*in*' will be used in place of '*on*'. Because the preposition - '*In*' is used after the verb- '*gap*'.

6. **(2)** The preposition-'*for*' will be used in place of '*since*'. Because '*Several years*' is a period of time but not '*a point of time*'.

7. **(3)** The preposition-'*to*' will be used in place of '*against*'. Because the preposition -'*to*' is used after the adjective-'*Prejudicial*'.

8. **(2)** '*Due to*' will not be used in the given sentence. Because use to, because and owing to are not used after '*the reason*'. While the reason..... that and the reason why......that are used. The Such as - The reason why She always remains ill is that she does not take care of her health.

9. **(1)** The preposition-'*at*' will be used after the verb - '*fired*'. Because fired at a person or fired at a thing is used.

10. **(3)** The preposition - '*till*' will not be used in the given sentence. Because the preposition- '*till*' is not necessary or suitable for the means of the given sentence.

11. **(4)** The preposition - '*in*' will be used in place of '*On*'. Because the preposition '*in*' is used before the noun-'*field*'.

12. **(1)** The preposition-'*of*' will not be used in the given sentence because the word despite itself has the meaning of '*inspite of*'i. Therefore, the preposition-'*of*' is not used after the word-'*despite*'.

13. **(4)** The preposition-'*over*' will be used in place of '*out*' because '*run over*' means '*To trample or to crush under the feet*'; to knock down. While '*run out*' means '*to come to an end*'. Therefore, '*Run over*' is suitable for the meaning of the given sentence. Such as-
    A school girl was run over by a car.
    Wheat stocks at the station shops are running out.

14. **(4)** The preposition - '*with*' will be used in place of '*at*'. because the preposition '*with*' is used with the verb -'*pleased*'.

15. **(3)** The preposition - '*with*' will be used in place of '*by*'. because the word-'*a cane opener*' has been used as an instrument or a tool in the given sentence. Therefore, the preposition-'*with*' is suitable for the given sentence.

16. **(2)** The preposition-'*to*' will be used after the verb-'*objected*' because the preposition '*to*' is always used after the verb - '*objected*'.

17. **(3)** The preposition-'*to*' will be used in place of '*for*' because the preposition-'*to*' is used after verb-'*invited*'.

18. **(2)** The phrasal verb-write off will be used in place of the phrasal verb-'*write of*' because the phrasal verb-'*write off*' means '*to end*' or '*to cancel a debt*' which is suitable for the meaning of the given sentence.

19. **(3)** The preposition - '*at*' will be used in place of '*by*' because the preposition-'*at*' is used after verb-'*amused*'.

20. **(2)** The preposition - '*at*' will be used in place of '*with*' because '*Angry at something or Angry with a person*' is used in English language.
    The preposition-'*at*' is suitable for the meaning of the given sentence.

CONJUNCTIONS

Conjunction :

A conjunction is a word which joins two or more than two words, phrases, clauses or sentences.

Look at these sentences:

Veena and Shweta went to market.
Mukesh gave me a book and an inkpot.
I went to see him but he was not there.
Give me tea or coffee.

Kinds of Conjunction

1. Co-ordinating conjunctions
2. Subordinating conjunctions

1. **Co-ordinating conjunctions :** And, but, or, nor, for, yet, so, as well as, either....... or, neither......nor, both........and, not only ...... but also, only, then, therefore, no less than, otherwise, or else, still, while/whereas, nevertheless etc are called coordinating conjunctions.

Co-ordinate means *'equal rank'*. The coordinating conjunctions are always used to join two equal ranking words, phrases, clauses and sentences or also used to join equal (=same) functioning words.

Look at these sentences

1. <u>Binay</u> and <u>Sudhir</u> were playing cricket.
   Noun   Noun
   Subject Subject
   └─────┬─────┘
      Two Subjects

2. <u>You</u> and <u>I</u> are students.
   Pronoun Pronoun
   Subject Subject
   └─────┬─────┘
      Two Subjects

3. <u>Veena</u> and <u>I</u> went to Vishnupur.
   Noun   Pronoun
   Subject Subject
   └─────┬─────┘
      Two Subjects

2. **Subordinating conjunctions :** As, Because, since, if, though, although, that, before, after, till, until, unless, whether, lest, as if, in case, so that, as long as, as soon as, which, when, where, why, how, as though etc are called Subordinating conjunctions.

Subordinate means *'dependent'* or *'depending on others'*. the subordinating conjunctions are used to join a subordinate clause to a principal clause.

Look at these sentences:

1. Bhavna was fined as she came late.
2. If he comes, I shall go.
3. Nilu is honest, though she is poor.
4. Although it was raining, I went out.
5. You will fail unless you work hard.

Kinds of subordinating conjunctions

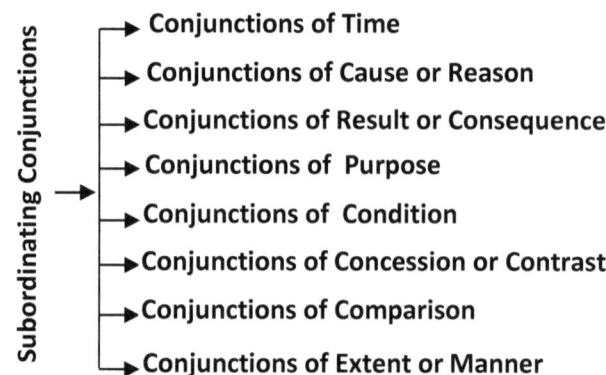

1. **Conjnctions of Time :** Thosee subordinating conjunctions which introduce adverb clauses of time are called conjunctions of time, as-

   Before : She had died before she reached twenty five.
   After : The doctor came after the patient had died.
   since : Many things have happened since I saw you.
   till/until : Wait here till/until I return.
   as soon as : I will leave as soon as you come.
   while : Make hay while the sun shines.
   so long as : His name will live so long as the world lasts.
   when : It happened when I was in Delhi.
   as : He found it as he was walking to college.
   Whenever : He comes to me whenever he needs money.

2. **Conjunctions of Cause or Reason:** Those subordinating conjunctions which introduce adverb clauses of cause or reason are called conjunctions of cause or reason, as -
   because : I love her because she loves me.
   since : He will go there since you desire it.
   as : As he was not there, I spoke to his brother.

3. **Conjunctions of Result or Consequence:** Those subordinating conjunctions which introduce adverb clauses of result or consequence are called conjunctions of result or consequence, as-
   That : He was so intelligent that he won the first prize.

4. **Conjunctions of purpose:** Those subordinating conjunctions which introduce adverb clauses of purpose are called conjunctions of purpose, as-
   That : We eat that we may live.
   so that : He worked hard so that he might pass.
   lest : Walk carefully lest you should fall.
   in order that : He works hard in order that he may become rich.

5. **Conjunctions of condition:** Those subordinating conjunctions which introduce adverb clauses of condition are called conjunctions of condition, as-
   If : He will dismiss you if you are late again.
   as if : She behaves as if she were mad.
   Unless : He can not be pardoned unless he confesses his fault.
   Provided/Provided that : I agree to these terms provided/provided that you agree to mine.

6. **Conjunctions of concession or contrast:** Those subordinating conjunctions which introduce adverb clauses of concession or contrast are called conjunctions of concession or contrast as-
   Although : He is an honest man although he is poor.
   Though : He is not contented though he is poor.
   however : He will never pass however hard he may try.

7. **Conjunctions of comparison:** Those subordinating conjunctions which introduce adverb clauses of comparison are called conjunctions of comparison as-
   as : He is as clever as I.
   He loves me as much as you.
   Than : She likes me no less than you.
   He is taller than you.

8. **Conjunctions of Extent or Manner:** Those subordinating conjunctions which introduce adverb clauses of extent or Manner are called conjunctions of extent or Manner as-
   As : Men will reap as they sow.
   according as : He chose the candidates according as they were fit.

Note : (i) Till, since, for after, but and before are used as prepositions or conjunctions.

	Conjunctions	Meaning
1.	and	*also, in addition to; added to; then; following this; as a result; (=aur)*
2.	as well as	*in addition to somebody/something;too; (=Aur bhi, Tatha)*
3.	otherwise	*used to state that the result would be if 5th did not happen or if the situation were different; apart from that; in a different way to the way mentioned; differently (=Nahi to)*
4.	or else	*if not; otherwise; used to introduce the second of the two possibilities; used to threaten or warn somebody (=Nahi to)*
5.	therefore (adv.)	*used to introduce the logical result of something that has just been mentioned; (-Atah, Isliye, Phaltah)*

VOCABULARY

6.	so (conj.)	used to show the reason fore something (=Atah, Isliye, Phaltah)
7.	hence (adv.)	for this reason (=Atah, Isliye, Phaltah)
8.	consequently (adv.)	as a result; therefore (=Atah, Isliye, Phaltah)
9.	either........or	used to show a choice of two things (=Ya to .....Ya)
10.	neither......nor	used to show that a negative statement is true of two things (=Na to ......Na)
11.	both........and	not only....but also (=Aur bhi)
12.	so.......that	is such a way that (=Itna......ki)
13.	too.....to	so......that (=Itna.....ki)
14.	so.....as	As......as (=Itna........Jitna ki)
15.	as........as	used when you are comparing two people or things, or two situations (=Itna.....Jitna ki)
16.	whether........or	one of the two; used to express a doubt or choice between two possibilities (=Chache.......Ya)
17.	as........so	as like that (Jaisa......Vaisa hi)
18.	as soon as	not losing anytime (=Jyonhi.....Tyonhi)
19.	but........	used to introduce a word or phrase that contrasts with what was said before (=Par, Parantu, Lekin, Magar, Kintu)
20.	or.......	used to introduce another possibility; used in negative sentences when mentioning two or more things (=Ya, Va, Athwa, Nahi to, Ki aur Na)
21.	no sooner......than	used to say that something happens immediately after something else (=Jyonhi.....Tyonhi)
22.	hardly.......when scarcely......when	to say that one thing happens immediately after another (Mushkil/Kathinta se......Ki)
23.		
24.	not only....but also	both......and (=Keval hi nahi.....Valki)
25.	where	in the place or situation in which (Jahan)
26.	wherever	in any place in all places that; every where; in all cases that; whenever (=Jahan kahin bhi)
27.	whence	from where (=Jahanse/Kahan se)
28.	when	at or during the time that; after; just after which;
29.	whenever	at any time that; everytime that; used when the time when something happens is not important (=Chahe kabhi, Jab chache, Kisi bhi awsa par)
30.	till or until	up to the point in time or the event mentioned (=Tab tak.....Jab tak)
31.	while	during the time that something is happening; when; at the same time as something else is happening; used to contrast two things (=Jab tak.......Tab tak)
32.	(a) because	for the reason that (=Kyonki)
	(b) because of (prep.)	on account of
33.	As	while something else is happening; in the way in which; used to state the reason for something; (=Kyonki)

34.	Since	from an event in the past until a later past event, or until now; because; as; (=Choonki)
35.	That	used after some verbs, adjectives and nouns to introduce a new part of the sentence; used to express a result; used for expressing a hope or a with (=Taki, Ki)
36.	lest	in order to prevent something from happening; used to introduce the reason for the particular emotion mentioned; in case (= Taki.....Na, Aisa na ho.....Ki)
37.	such......that	used to say that one thing can, will or might happen or be true, depending on another thing happening or being tue; when; whether; every time; (=Ydi)
38.	if	used to say that something can only happen or be true in a particular situation; used to give the only situation in which something will not happen or be tue; if not (Jab tak ......Tab tak, Ydi......Nahi)
39.	unless	used to say what must happen or be done to make it possible for something else to happen; if (=Basharte ki)
40.	provided	In a way that suggests something as it would be if; that (=Mano ki/ Vishay Mai, Bare Mai)
41.	as if / as though	used for introducing a statement that makes the main statement in a sentence seem surprising;- - though; used to mean 'but' or 'however' when you are commenting on a statement; In spite of the fact that; even though. (=Ydyapi......Phir bhi/Tathapi)
42.	although	despite the fact that; although; used to add a fact or an opinion that makes the previous statement less strong or less important (=Ydyapi......Phir bhi/Tathapi)
43.	though	used with an adjective or adverb to mean 'to whatever degree'; In whatever way; used to introduce a statement that contrasts with something that has just been said. (=Chahe....Kitni hi)
44.	however	used to say that something happens in the same way; used to introduce a statement that contrasts with something that has just been said. (=Chahe......Kitni hi)
45.	as.......as	used to say that something happens in the same way (=Utna......Jitna)
46.	no less than	used to emphasize a large amount (=Apekshakrit kam nahi)
47.	whereas	used to compare or contrast two facts; used at the beginning of a sentence in an official document to mean 'because of' the fact that.......(=Virodhi Bhawna Mai, Jabki)

VOCABULARY

48.	nevertheless	despite something that you have just mentioned; none the less (=Tathapi, To bhi)	54.	not yet	and not even now (=Abhi nahi)
49.	how (adv)	In what way or manner; used to ask about somebody's health; used before an adjective or adverb to ask about the amount or degree to ask about the amount or degree etc of something or about somebody's age; used to express surprise or pleasure etc; (=Kaise, Kis prakar)	55.	yet (conj)	even then; nevertheless (=Phir bhi)
			56.	as (conj)	when, while; since, seeing that (=Tab, us samay)
			57.	as to	about, concerning (=Vishay mai)
			58.	so as to	in order to (=Is vajah se)
			59.	as far as	so long as (=Jahan tak)
			60.	as (adv)	in the same degree (=Usi prakar se, Utna)
50.	however (adv.) howsoever	in whatever way or degree (=Kuchchh Bhi ho, Ydyapi, Kitna bhi)	61.	as now	Just at this time (= Isi samay)
			62.	as then	Just at that time (=Usi samay)
51.	however (conj.) howsoever	all the same, nevertheless (Tathapi, Baharhal)	63.	as yet	So far, upto this time (=Abhi Tak)
			64.	as regards/As to	in connection with (=Bare Mai, Sambanth Mai, Vishay Mai)
52.	yet (adv)	by this or that time; so far; upto this time; still (=Ab tak, Tab tak, Abhi tak, Abtak bhi)	65.	a compared with	in comparison to (=Ki tulna mai)
53.	as yet	up to now (=Is samay tak)	66.	as for this	in respect of, in this connection (=is Vishay Mai)

ENGLISH

PRACTICE SET

Q.1. *Find out the error part of the following sentences:*

1. Both Shyam (1) / as well as Ghanshyam (2) / are interested to (3) / prepare the examination. (4)/No error (5)

2. Scarcely had I bought (1) / the ticket than (2) / the postmaster showed (3) / the green flag. (4) / No error (5)

3. I asked him (1) / that why he was (2) / not preparing for the (3) /U.P.S.C. examination. (4) / No error (5)

4. Fifteen years (1) / have passed (2) / that he came back (3) / from Darbhanga. (4) / No error (5)

5. In Bihar leaders are (1) / taking bad advantage of casteism (2) / I think it is (3) / nothing than bad things. (4) / No error (5)

6. The criminal had (1) / hardly put the precious things (2) / in his bag than (3) / the landlord got up. (4) / No error (5)

7. Either you (1) / and he (2) / went there (3) / to see the helpless. (4) / No error (5)

8. While I opened (1) / the gate of my house, (2) / I found (3) / a dead cat. (4) / No error (5)

9. No sooner did the jeep arrive (1) / at the station (2) / then a young police officer (3) / jumped out of it. (4) / No error (5)

10. His book has been (1) / missing from (2) / his room (3) / since yesterday. (4) / No error (5)

11. I have never (1) / visited (2) / nor intend to visit (3) / foreign countries. (4) / No error (5)

12. His manners indicate (1) / thath he has no other intention (2) / than (3) / to steal his money. (4) / No error (5)

13. The headmaster advised the student (1) / who had failed in the examination twice (2) / that not to attempt it again (3) / until he had time to prepare for it properly. (4) / No error (5)

14. Nishant could not (1) / go to the picnic (2) / for his mother (3) / was not well. (4) / No error (5)

15. He says he (1) / is going to (2) / cut down (3) / his smoking. (4) / No error (5)

16. When learning to swim (1) / one of the most important things (2) / is to relax (3) / No error. (4)

17. He not only comes here (1) / for swimming but also for coaching (1) / new swimmers. (4) / No error (5)

18. A more irrational world (1) / to this one in which (2) / we presently live (3) / could hardly be conceived. (4) / No error (5)

19. Hardly had (1) / I left the house (2) / than it began (3) / to rain. (4) / No error (5)

20. You should take (1) / a book with you (2) / unless (3) / you have to wait. (4) / No error (5)

Q.2 *Correct the following sentences:*

1. While the cock crew, the farmer woke up.

2. When the leader was speaking, the people were listening carefully.

3. She works hard until she will fail in the examination.

4. His friend was not only fined and also sent to jail.

5. He plays neither cricket or football.

6. He inquired that where was the college.

7. Two weeks have passed before he came here.

8. The crops will dry since the rains fall.

9. He asked me that whether Mukesh had gone.

10. Take care unless you should fall.

11. Unless you do not apologize, I shall punish you.

12. No sooner does Mukesh arrive then he begins to study.

13. He would have the book rather but the note book.
14. I have no other hobby but that of collecting books.
15. He visited not only Mumbai also Kolkata.
16. Scarcely had she left than a storm began to blow.
17. No sooner had the fight started but Mohan fled away.
18. He is poor, yet he is honest.
19. He returned his residence before the sun had set.
20. Work hard or you will fail.

Q.3 *Fill in the blanks with suitable conjunctions (connectors/subordinators):*

1. He was tired, ..., he went home.
2. Do you know..........he was.
3. ....you apologize, I shall punish you.
4. Two months have passed........he left college.
5. He ran hard ...... he should miss the train.
6. I had no other hobby .... that of collecting books.
7. He would have the mobile set rather..........the motorcycle.
8. No sooner had the fight begun ....he ran away.
9. Scarcely had he left .... a storm began to blow.
10. I have neither written to her....... spoken to her.
11. He visited not only Delhi........Rajgir.
12. My daughter won both a prize.......a scholarship.
13. Either my brother was there......my son-in-law was there.
14. He is slow......he is steady.
15. ......there is life, there is hope.
16. I have never seen him......that unfortunate event happened.
17. Man proposes........God disposes.
18. Though he slay me,........I will trust him.
19. Time.......tide wait for no man.
20. Give me something to drink,........I shall die of thirst.

ENGLISH

ANSWERS WITH EXPLANATION

Q.1.
1. (2) 'And' will be used in place of 'as well as because 'Both.............and' is used.
2. (2) 'When' will be used in place of 'than' because 'Scarcely ....when' is used.
3. (2) 'That' will not be used in the given sentence because the conjunction -'that' is not before the Interrogative words such as why, how, when, where, who, whom, what, which ....etc.
4. (3) The conjunction -'Since' will be used in place of 'that', because 'Since' is used in the sense of 'Jab se...........Tab se' as a conjunction.
5. (4) 'Nothing but' will be used in place of 'Nothing than'
6. (3) 'When' will be used in place of 'than' because 'hardly..........when' is used.
7. (2) 'Or' will be used in place of 'and' because 'Either..........or' is used.
8. (1) 'When' will be used in place of 'while'. Read the rules for special knowledge.
9. (3) 'Than' will be used in place of 'than' because 'No sooner ....than' is used.
10. (5) Given sentence is correct.
11. (3) 'Or' will be used in place of 'nor'. 'Or' is used after 'not' and 'never' but 'nor' is not used after 'not' and 'never'.
12. (3) 'But' will be used in place of 'than'.
13. (3) 'That' will not be used because it is not essential for the meaning of the given sentence.
14. (3) 'Because' will be used in place of 'for'.
15. (1) 'That' will be used after 'he says'
16. (1) 'While' will be used in place of 'when'.
17. (1) 'He comes here not only' will be used in place of 'He not only comes here'.
18. (2) 'Than' will be used in place of 'to' because 'than' is used after comparative degree.
19. (3) 'When' will be used in place of 'than' because 'when' is used after 'hardly'.
20. (3) 'In case' will be used in place of 'unless' because 'In case' will be express precaution (=carefulness) but 'unless' is not used to express precaution.

Q.2.
1. When the cock crew, the farmer woke up.
2. While the leader was speaking, the people were listening carefully.
3. She works hard unless she will fail in the examination.
4. His friends was not only fined but also sent to jail.
5. He plays neither cricket nor football.
6. He inquired where the college was.
7. Two weeks have passed since he came here.
8. The crops will have dried before the rains fall.
9. He asked me whether Mukesh had gone.
10. Take care lest you should fall.
11. Unless you apologize, I shall punish you.
12. No sooner doe Mukesh arrive than he begins to study.
13. He would have the book rather than the note-book.
14. I have no other hobby than that of collecting books.
15. He visited not only Mumbai but also Kolkata.
16. Scarcely had she left when a storm began to blow.
17. No sooner had the fight started than Mohan fled away.
18. Though he is poor, yet he is honest.
19. He returned to his residence after the sun had set.
20. Work hard otherwise/else you will fail.

Q.3.

1. therefore	2. who	3. unless
4. since	5. lest	6. than
7. than	8. than	9. when
10. nor	11. but also	12. and
13. or	14. but	15. While
16. since	17. and	18. yet
19. and	20. Else	

TENSE

KINDS OF TENSE

1. Present Tense
2. Past Tense
3. Future Tense

1. **Present Tense** : An action which is done at the present time is in Present Tense.
   In other words- A verb that refers to present time is said to be in the Present Tense; as,
   1. I read a book.
   2. I am reading a book.

2. **Past Tense** : An action which is done at the past time is in Past Tense.
   In other words - A verb that refers to past time is said to be in the Past Tense; as,
   1. I wrote a letter.
   2. I was writing a letter.

3. **Future Tense** : An action which will be done at the future time is in Future Tense.
   In other words - A verb that refers to future time is said to be in the Future Tense; as,
   1. I shall write a letter.
   2. I shall be writing a letter.
   The examples given above show that the tense- present, past and future Tense also have four subdivisions.

1. **Present Tense**
   There are four subdivisions of Present Tense.
   1. Present Indefinite Tense/Simple Present Tense
   2. Present Imperfect/Continuous/Progressive Tense

1. **Simple Present Tense**
   Structure : S+ M.V^1/ M.V^5 + O
   Use of Simple Present Tense

   Rule (1) : Simple Present Tense is used to express habitual or regular or repeated action; as,
   Mukesh goes to bed at 10 p.m.
   He always comes here on Sunday.
   she reads a newspaper every morning.

   Rule (2) : This tense (Simple Present Tense) is used to express universal truth, principle and permanent activities; as,
   The sun rises in the east.
   Two and two makes four.
   Man is mortal.

   Rule (3) : This tense (Simple Present Tense) is used to express possession; as,
   This pen belongs to me.
   I have a car.

   Rule (4) : This Tense (Simple Present Tense) is used to express mental activity, emotions and feelings; as,
   We believe in God.
   He understands my problem.

   Rule (5) Simple Present Tense is used to express fixed program me or fixed plan of Future time. It denotes future time; as,
   The college reopens in October.

   Meaning : (= The college will reopen in October.)
   He goes to Chennai next month.
   Meaning : (= He will go to Chennai next month.)

   She leaves for New York next Monday.
   Meaning : (= She will leave for New York next Monday.)
   The Prime Minister comes here tomorrow.
   Meaning : (= The Prime Minister will come here tomorrow.)
   My brother returns tomorrow.
   Meaning : (= My brother will return tomorrow.)

2. **Present Continuous Tense**
   Structure : S + is/are/am + M.V.^{4} + O
   Use of Present Continuous Tense

   Rule (1) : Present Continuous Tense is used for an action going on (continued) at the time of speaking; as,
   Mukesh is coming now.
   They are playing.
   The girls are playing kho-kho.

Rule (2) : Present Continuous Tense is used for a temporary action which may not be actually happening at the time of speaking. But that action is continued in these days or near about the suitable time; as,

I am living in a rented house.

He is reading the Mahabharata.

In the sentences given above, the actions (verbs) such as- living, reading and studying are not happening (continued) at the time of speaking but these actions are happening nowadays or near about the suitable time.

Rule (3) : This tense (Present Continuous Tense) is used for a fixed program me or plan of the nearest future (time); as,

He is going to Chennai tonight.

She is going home tomorrow.

Rule (4) : This tense (Present Continuous Tense) is used to denote (express) intention or likelihood. It denotes the sense of future time; as,

I am going to see my father-in-law. -Intention

He is going to die.   -Likelihood

Rule (5) : The following verbs are not used in Present Continuous Tense such as - See, hear, smell, notice, recognize, taste, appear, seem, look, love, hate, abhor, despise, detest, like, dislike, hope, doubt, admit, accept, refuse, deny, prefer, regard, satisfy, want, with, desire, intend, please, displease, mean, suppose, think, imagine, presuppose, recall, recollect, remember, forget, believe, know, trust, own, possess, have, belong to, keep, consist of, contain, comprise, include, involve, equal, cost, deserve, depend, fit, owe, lack, require, resemble, need, dare, sound............ etc. as;

She is knowing him very well.   (×)

She knows him very well.   (√)

He is understanding it.   (×)

He understands it.   (√)

3. **Present Perfect Tense**

Structure : S + has/have + M.V.^{3} + O

Use of Present Perfect Tense

Rule (1) : Present Perfect Tense is used to indicate/ denote (express) completed activities (actions) in the immediate past; as,

She has written a letter.

I have just bought a pen.

He has gone to patna market.

Rule (2) : This tense (=present prefect tense) is used to express the past actions which are continued in the present time (or their effect is in the present time); as,

He has cut his finger.

Meaning : (= and it is bleeding now)

She has finished her work.

Meaning : (= now she is free)

My daughter has ate all the apples.

Meaning : (= there aren't any left for you.)

It is obvious from the sentences given above that the actions have been completed in past but their effect is continued in the present time.

Rule (3) : This tense (=present perfect tense) is used to denote (=express) an action starting (=beginning) at sometime in the past and continuing (=going on) up to the present moment. The preposition - for/since is used with such actions according to need; as,

I have lived in this house since 1999.Meaning : (= Now also I am living in this house.)

He has taught in this school for five years.

Meaning : (= Now also he is teaching in this school.)

She has been ill since Friday.

Meaning : (= Now also he is ill.)

Rule (4) : This tense (=present perfect tense) is used to express the past actions which have been completed (=or finished) in the past time, but their time is not given and not definite (=is definitely unknown); as,

She has gone to America.

Have you read ' The Arabian Night'?

Rule (5) : Present Perfect Tense is never used with the past time expressing words (=Adverbs of past time) such as- last year, last week, last month, yesterday, the other day, ago etc. While (=whereas) simple past tense is used with the past time expressing words (=Adverbs of past time); as,

I have seen him last year.	(×)
I saw him last year.	(√)
He has arrived last week.	(×)
He arrived last week.	(√)

Rule (6) : Present Prefect Tense is used with the following Adverbs or adverbial phrases such as, ever, never, always occasionally, often, several times, already, yet (=in negatives and questions), just, lately, recently, so far, upto, upto now, upto the present, since, for, today, this week, this month, during the last few weeks, during the last few years etc; as,

He has come recently.	(√)
She has not gone yet.	(√)

4. **Present Perfect Continuous Tense**
   Structure : S +has been/have been + M.V.^{4} + Object + for/since + time
   Use of Present Perfect Continuous Tense

   Rule (1) : Present Perfect Continuous Tense is used for an action which began at some time in the past and is still Continuing; as,
   She has been reading a novel since morning.
   It has not been raining since last Monday.
   Guriya has been singing a song for an hour.
   I have been teaching in the school for five years.

   Rule (2) : This tense (Present Perfect Continuous Tense) is used for an action which began at sometime in the past and continued for some time. It has been temporarily closed or finished at this time (moment). But its effect is also continuing now; as.
   She has been crying.
   Why have your clothes been so wet?
   I have been watering the gardens.

2. **Past Tense**
   There are four subdivisions of Past Tense :
   1. Past Indefinite Tense/Simple Past Tense
   2. Past Imperfect / Continuous / Progressive Tense
   3. Past Perfect Tense
   4. Past Perfect Continuous Tense

1. **Simple Past Tense**
   Structure : S + M.V^2 + O
   Use of Simple Past Tense
   Rule (1) : Simple Past Tense is used for an action which completed at some certain time in the past; as,
   He went to Mumbai yesterday.
   She came to see me last night.

   Look at these sentences :
   1. He received her letter a month ago.
   2. I left college last year.
   3. The ship sailed yesterday.

   Rule (2) : This tense (simple past tense) is used for an action which completed (occurred) in the past time. In this case, it is used without an adverb of time; as,
   The peon bought a cup of coffee.
   His father came back.
   I bought this pen in New York.

   Rule (3) : Simple Past Tense (This tense) is used to express past habitual actions (for past habits); as,
   He went on Sunday.
   In my childhood, I played cricket.

   Rule (4) : Simple Past Tense is used after the phrasal expressions such as - 'it is time', 'it is high time', 'it is about time', etc; as,
   It is time he started playing cricket.
   It is high time she left for the bus stop.

   Rule (5) : simple Past Tense is used to express a situation related to past time; as,

It was night.	She was very ill.
I was helpless.	He was very poor.
It was summer.	It was March.

Rule (6) : If the adverbs of time such as - today, this morning, this evening, this week, this month, this year, recently... etc. are used in a sentence, Simple Past Tense or Present Perfect Tense can be used in the sentence; as,

He saw me today.
He has seen me today.
He saw me this week.
He has seen me this week.

Rule (7) : Simple Past Tense is used to express an action to be done in the past; as,
While she cooked, I wrote a book.
While they played, we studied.
When my daughter played, I worked.

Rule (8) : Suppositional sentences often start (begin) with the word - If, as if, as though, if only, I wish, we wish, he wishes, she wishes, they wish... etc. simple past tense is used with the suppositional sentences; as,
I wish I were the Chief Minister of Bihar.
If I became the Prime Minister of India, I would solve the problem of Kashmir.
He talks as if he were my master.

Rule (9) : Simple Past Tense is used in the If - clause of conditional sentence. It denotes present or future time; as,
If you reached in time, you might catch the train.
If my servant came on time, I would pay him his wages.

Rule (10) : When the Reporting Verb in the direct speech is in past tense and the reported speech is in simple present tense, The Simple Present Tense of the Reported speech is changed into simple past tense in the Indirect speech; as,

He said, "I want to read a novel."   Direct
He said that he wanted to read a novel. Indirect

But when the Reporting Verb in the direct speech is in past tense and the universal truth, principle and proverb are used in the Reported Speech, The tense of the reported speech is not changed in the Indirect speech because simple Present Tense is used with the universal truth, principle and proverb; as,
He said, "Two and two makes four."
　　　Direct
He said that two and two makes four.
　　　Indirect (√)
He said that two and two make four.
　　　　　(×)

Rule (11) : When any action (An action) is continued in the past and any other action takes place (occurs) during the continued action, Past Continuous Tense is used for the continued action and Simple Past Tense is used for the action taking place (occurring) during the continued action; as,
When I was writing a book, Sudhir Ji arrived.
She was cooking food when her husband came.
While he was watering the plants, an insect bit him.
While the girls were dancing, their father came to see them.

Rule (12) : The two actions took place in the past, out of these two actions, The first action took place first and the second action took place next. The first action is called previous action and Past Perfect Tense is used with the previous Action. But the second action is called subsequent action and Simple Past Tense is used with the subsequent action; as,

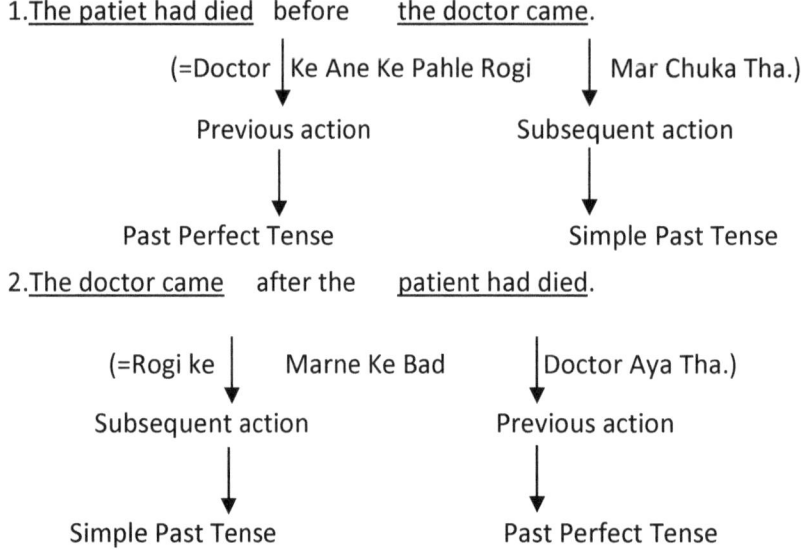

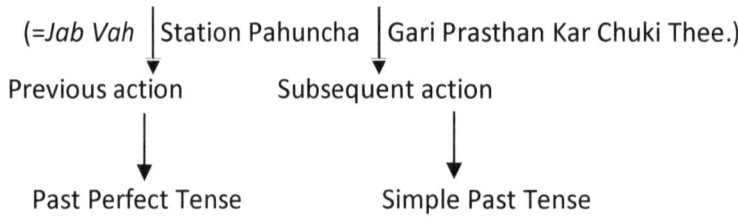

2. **Past Continuous Tense**

    Structure : S + was/were + M.V^4 + O

    Use of Past Continuous Tense

    Rule (1) : Past Continuous Tense is used to express (denote) an action going at sometime in the past. The time of the action may or may not be indicated; as

    I was writing this book yesterday morning.

    She saw me as she was passing by yesterday.

    Rule (2) : When the Reporting verb in the direct speech is in past tense and the reported speech is in Present Continuous Tense, The Present Continuous Tense of the Reported Speech is changed into Past Continuous Tense in the Indirect speech; as,

    Veena said, " I am going to Bishnupur." Direct

    Veena said that she was going to Bishnupur.

                                              Indirect

    Rule (3) : When the two actions are taking place (continued) at the same time in the past, Past Continuous Tense is used for both actions; as,

    While my mother was singing, I was sleeping

    While I was writing this chapter, my wife was watching T.V.

    Rule (4) : When the verbs - *'get'*, *'become'* and *'grow'* are used to express (denote) gradual Increase or decrease in any action in the past, Past Continuous Tense is used with them; as,

    He was becoming poorer and poorer.

    She was becoming more and more beautiful.

3. **Past Perfect Tense**

    Structure : S + had + M.V.^{3} + O

    Use of Past Perfect Tense

    Rule (1) : If the two actions took place in the past, out of these two actions, the first action has complete first and the second action has completed next, the first completed action is called previous action and past perfect tense is

used with it (the previous action) and the second completed action which happened next is called subsequent action and simple past tense is used with it (the subsequent action); as,
The crops had destroyed before it rained.
(= *Varsha Hone se Pahle Phasal Nast Ho Chuka Tha.*)

Rule (2) : When the reporting verb in the direct speech is in past tense and the reported speech is in present tense, The Present Perfect Tense is changed into past perfect tense in the Indirect Speech; as,
Direct : He said, "I have finished my work."
Indirect : He said that he had finished his work.

Rule (3) : When the reporting verb in the direct speech is in past tense and the reported speech is in simple past tense, The Simple Past Tense is changed into Past Perfect Tense in the Indirect Speech; as,
Direct : Mukesh said, "I bought a pen yesterday.
Indirect : Mukesh said that he had bought a pen the previous day.

Rule (4) : Past Perfect Tense in used to describe the unreal situations (suppositional facts) after these phrasal expressions - I wish, we wish, he wishes, she wishes, they wish, as if, as though.......etc; as,
She wishes she had been born in 1948.
She talks to me as if she had come from the film industry.

Rule (5) : Past Perfect Tense is used in the following structure to describe the unreal situations (suppositional facts):

Structure:
(i) If + S + had + M.V^3 + (,) + S + would/could/might + have + M.V^3 + O + (.)
(ii) Had + S + M.V^3 + (,) + S + would/could/might + have + M.V^3 + O + (.); as,
If the police had come a little before, the criminal would not have gone away.
Had the student studied honestly, he would have succeeded.

Rule (6) : Such sentences whose two parts do not look obviously. The second action is understood in such sentences. it seems (appears) that the first action had finished much earlier the second action. Past Perfect Tense is used to express the first action; as,
Binay had never gone to Delhi before.
(= *Binay Isase Pahle Delhi Nahi Gaya Tha*)

4. **Past Perfect Continuous Tense**
Structure : S + had been + MV^4 + O + for/since + time.
Use of Past Perfect Continuous Tense
Rule (1) : Past Perfect Continuous Tense is used for an action that began before a certain point in the past and continued upto that time; as,
His elder sister had been dancing for two hours.
I had been reading a novel since 2013.
She had been singing a song.
My younger brother had been quarrelling.

Rule (2) : If the reporting verb in the direct speech is in past tense and the reported speech is in Present Perfect Continuous Tense, The Present Perfect Continuous Tense is changed into Past Perfect Continuous Tense in the Indirect Speech; as,
Veena said, "I have been watching T.V. for two hours.? *Direct*
Veena said that she had been watching T.V. for two hours. *Indirect*

Rule (3) : If the reporting verb in the Direct Speech is in Past Tense and the reported speech is in Past Continuous Tense, The Past Continuous Tense is changed into Past Perfect Countinuous Tense in the Indirect Speech; as,
Binay said, " I was working in the office."
Direct
Binday said that he had been working in the office. *Indirect*
Mr. Thakur said to me "You were trying to disturbed me." *Direct*
Mr. Thakur told me that I had been trying to disturb him. *Indirect*

3. **Future Tense**

There are four subdivisions of Future Tense.

1. Future Indefinite Tense/Simple Future Tense
2. Future Imperfect/Continuous/Progressive Tense
3. Future Perfect Tense
4. Future Perfect Continuous Tense

1. **Simple Future Tense**

Structure : S + Shall / will + M.V^1 + O

Use of Simple Future Tense

Rule (1) : Simple Future Tense is used for an action which will be happened (taken place) in future (in coming time); as,

He will help you.

You will go to college tomorrow.

My brother will be twenty-five next year.

She will arrive at 6 o' clock.

Rule (2) : Simple Future Tense is used with the Principal Clause of Conditional Sentence; as,

I shall buy a motorcycle	when the price comes down.
Principal Clause	Subordinate Clause
Simple Future Tense	Simple Present Tense
If you come here	I shall help you.
Subordinate Clause	Principal Clause
Simple Present Tense	Simple Future Tense

Rule (3) : The following structures are used to express the actions taking place (happening) in future; as,

(a) *Subject + has/have + Infinitive (to + V^1)*; as,

I have to pay the fees. - (future time)

She has to do this work at any cost.

(b) *Subject + is/are/am + Infinitive (to + V^1)*; as,

He is to come to Patna.

You are to appear at the examination.

2. **Future Continuous Tense**

Structure : S + Shall/ will + be + M.V^4 + O

Use of Future Continuous Tense

Rule (1) : Future Continuous Tense is used to express an action going on at some time in future time; as,

He will be playing cricket tomorrow morning.

She will be staying there.

Rule (2) : Future Continuous Tense is used to express a certain (definite) programme or plan of future; as,

Manisha will be meeting me tomorrow.

Binay will be staying there till Friday.

3. **Future Perfect Tense**

Structure : S + Shall/ will + have + M.V^3 + O

Use of Future Perfect Tense

Rule (1) : Future Perfect Tense is used to indicate the completion of an action by a certain future time; as,

His brother will have finished the work by next month.

She will have come back home by evening.

He will have finished his work before Monday.

Rule (2) : Future Perfect Tense is used to express likelihood (possibility) or Inference (Guess), its relation is with the past; as,

You will have heard the name of Mother Teresa.

You will have read the Gita.

He will have watched the film, Mother India.

PRACTICE SET

Q.1 Pick out the verbs and state their tense:

1. Her mother died when she was quite young.
2. He slept well last night.
3. She will learn to write English in a year.
4. The cat lay on the floor.
5. We go to school at 10 O' clock.
6. I met her last Friday.
7. I spend the afternoon at the tuition centre.
8. A mad elephant killed the baby.
9. An aero plane flies in the air.
10. I have lost my pen.
11. The light has gone out.
12. I know his father and mother.
13. He never tells a lie.
14. The peon rings the bell.
15. He wore black shirt.
16. The dog barked at night.
17. She want to Mumbai yesterday.
18. Mohan failed in class X last year.
19. I shall go to Jamshedpur tomorrow.
20. I forget his name.

Q.2 Fill in the blanks with suitable forms of the verbs given in the *brackets*:

1. He ..... to college everyday. **(goes/going)**
2. My young brother .... to Mumbai last month **(go/went)**
3. He .... from fever since last night. **(has suffered/has been suffering)**
4. He .... just now. **(has arrived/arrived)**
5. I ...... working for two hours. **(has been/am)**
6. I .... in Patna since 1993. **(have lived/lived)**
7. The Mughals .... The battle of Panipat. **(have won/won)**
8. Stephenson ...... the steam engine. **(has invented/invented)**
9. Mahatma Gandhi .... in 1948. **(has died / died)**
10. She ...... before her husband came. **(has died / died)**
11. The train had left before they ..... the station **(reached/will reach)**
12. They will play cricket if the principal .... them. **(allows/allowed)**
13. He...... a letter yet. **(has not written/ did not write)**
14. When I .... my work, I shall take rest. **(finished/finish)**
15. He told me that she..... for seven days. **(had been ill/was ill)**
16. Bhavna will have reached home before the sun....... **(will set/sets)**
17. Ajit and Rekha .... to the cinema last night. **(have gone/went)**
18. It .... for five hours. **(has been raining/is raining)**
19. Five plus five .... ten. **(make/makes)**
20. My elder daughter ...... born in 2002. **(was/is)**
21. I .... the Red Fort. **(have never seen/never saw)**
22. Does he .... fast? **(run/runs)**
23. The Earth .... round the Sun. **(moved/moves)**
24. Who......... the Taj Mahal? **(builds/built)**
25. She..... that film already. **(has seen/saw)**

VOCABULARY

26. How did they ...... to Jajur ? (come/came)
27. Tendulkar generally........very well. (plays/played)
28. But today he .... very badly. (is playing/plays)
29. The Sun..... in the east. (rises/rose)
30. I was born in 1972. I first ...... to college in 1986. (had gone/went)

Q.3 Rewrite the following sentences after correcting errors:

1. She does not write to me for two weeks.
2. Vikas has been eating apples since he is a child.
3. You didn't yet see the Governor.
4. He is away from school since August last.
5. He said that the college was closed since last Friday.
6. Five hours have passed since he had fallen asleep.
7. Eight years passed since his grandfather died.
8. Two months have passed since I have come here.
9. She is long known to me.
10. My father will reach there by this time tomorrow.
11. I am sorry for the students who failed in the examination.
12. He will come when he will be ready.
13. She will write as soon as she will arrive soon.
14. It's high time (that) you go home.
15. It's time (that) we play cricket.
16. He is often asking himself questions.
17. He is born in India.
18. She has been born in a town.
19. If I was a king, I would be happy.
20. I finished my work just now.
21. He was ill for two days when the doctor was sent for.
22. They come here a month ago.
23. She watches television now.
24. The great reformer had died in 1948.
25. We shall serve you if you will come.

Q.4 Select the correct form of the verb shown in brackets in each sentence and write it in the the brackets opposite:

1. He $\begin{Bmatrix}(a) went \\ (b) has\ gone\end{Bmatrix}$ to Muzaffarpur yesterday. ( )

2. She $\begin{Bmatrix}(a)\ is \\ (b) has\ been\end{Bmatrix}$ doing her home work for an hour. ( )

3. I shall teach you if you $\begin{Bmatrix}(a) come \\ (b) will\ come\end{Bmatrix}$ ( )

4. I shall teach you if you $\begin{Bmatrix}(a) come \\ (b) will\ come\end{Bmatrix}$ ( )

5. My grandmother $\begin{Bmatrix}(a) told \\ (b) has\ told\end{Bmatrix}$ me a story just now ( )

6. The Rajadhani Express $\begin{Bmatrix}(a) has\ left \\ (b) left\end{Bmatrix}$ an hour ago. ( )

7. He felt that he $\begin{Bmatrix}(a)\ will \\ (b)\ would\end{Bmatrix}$ resign his post. ( )

8. She had gone to college when I $\begin{Bmatrix}(a) had\ come \\ (b) come\end{Bmatrix}$ to see her. ( )

9. The boys will play if the headmaster $\begin{Bmatrix}(a) allows \\ (b)\ allowed\end{Bmatrix}$ them. ( )

10. It $\begin{Bmatrix}(a) is\ raining \\ (b) has\ been\ raining\end{Bmatrix}$ all day. ( )

Q.5 Find out the error part of the following sentences:

1. If Manali had (1)/worked hard (2) / she will have got the job (3)/she desired. (4) / No error (5)

2. He told me (1)/ that he wrote a letter (2) / to his superior (3)/ for a certain reason. (4) / No error (5)

3. I am working (1)/ at my present job (2) / since the day (3)/ a son was born to my brother. (4) / No error (5)

4. After Ravi (1)/ read the magazines and newspapers, (2) / and watched T.V. Programme, (3)/ he decided to go out and meet some old friends (4) / No error (5)

5. His father would have been pleased (1)/ to get him a wrist watch (2) / if he would have worked (3)/ harder and secured higher marks in the university examination. (4) / No error (5)

6. When the doctors found (1)/ that the player has taken (2) / prohibited medicines, he reported (3)/ the matter to the team manager. (4) / No error (5)

7. As soon as (1)/ the clock strike five (2) / they down tools (3)/ and off they go. (4) / No error (5)

8. It had been our custom (1)/ from immemorial time to be (2) / hospitable to those who come to our doors. (3)/ No error (4)

9. I asked (1)/ if she has looked everywhere (2) / and she said, 'yes'. (3) /No error (4)

10. Had I realised (1)/ that it was such a long way (2) / I would take a taxi. (3) /No error (4)

11. As he dived from the spring board (1)/ he was terrified to see (2) / that the water was drained from the pool the previous night. (3) / No error (4)

12. As I am suffering from fever since morning (1)/ I shall not be able to attend the function (2) / You are going to organise this (3) /No error (4)

13. She wishes (1)/ that she has studied literature instead of history (2)/when she was in college. (3) /No error (4)

14. Much water (1)/ has flown (2) / under the bridge since then. (3) /No error (4)

15. I do not wish (1)/ to rise (2) / false hopes. (3) /No error (4)

Answers With Explanation

Q.1.

1.	died was	Past tense	(simple)
2.	slept	Past tense	(simple)
3.	will	Future tense	(simple)
4.	lay	Past tense	(simple)
5.	go	Present tense	(simple)
6.	met	Past tense	(simple)
7.	spend	Present tense	(simple)
8.	killed	Past tense	(simple)
9.	flies	Present tense	(simple)
10.	have lost	Present tense	(perfect)
11.	has gone out	Present tense	(perfect)
12.	know	Present tense	(simple)
13.	tells	Present tense	(simple)
14.	rings	Present tense	(simple)
15.	wore	Past tense	(simple)
16.	barked	Past tense	(simple)
17.	went	Past tense	(simple)
18.	failed	Past tense	(simple)
19.	shall go	Future tense	(simple)
20.	forget	Present tense	(simple)

Q.2.

1. goes
2. Went
3. has been suffering
4. has arrived
5. have been
6. have lived
7. won
8. invented
9. died
10. had died
11. reached
12. allows
13. has not written
14. finish
15. had been ill
16. sets
17. went
18. has been raining
19. makes
20. was
21. have never seen
22. run
23. moves
24. built
25. has seen
26. come
27. plays
28. is playing
29. rises
30. went

Q.3.

1. She has not written to me for two weeks.
2. Vikas has been eating apples since he was a child.
3. You haven't seen the Governor yet.
4. He has been away from school since August last.
5. He said that the college had been closed since last Friday.
6. Five hours have passed since he fell asleep.
7. Eight years have passed since his grandfather died.
8. Two months have passed since I came here.
9. She has been long known to me.
10. My father will have reached there by this time tomorrow.
11. I am sorry for the students who have failed in the examination.
12. He will come when he is ready.
13. She will write as soon as she arrives soon.
14. It's high time (that) you went home.
15. It's time (that) we played cricket.
16. He often asks himself questions.
17. He was born in India.
18. She was born in a town.
19. If I were a king, I would be happy.
20. I have finished my work just now.
21. He had been ill for two days when the doctor was sent for.
22. They came here a month ego.
23. She is watching television now.
24. The great reformer died in 1948.
25. We shall serve you if you come.

Q.4.

1. (a) went
2. (b) has been
3. (a) come
4. (a) goes
5. (b) has told
6. (b) left
7. (b) would
8. (b) came
9. (a) allows
10. (b) has been raining

ENGLISH

Q.5.

1. (3) 'Would have' will be used in place of 'will have'. The Structure –
   'If + subject + had + M.V³ + (,) + subject + would have + M.V³ + object' is used in English Language.

2. (2) 'He had written a letter' will be used in place of ' he wrote a letter'.

3. (1) 'I have been working' will be used in place of 'I am working'.

4. (2) 'Had read' will be used in place of 'read'. The structure - 'Subject + M.V² + object + after + subject + had + M.V³ + object' is used in English language; as,
   The doctor came after the patient had died. (✓)
   After the patient had died, the doctor came. (✓)
   The doctor came after the patient died. (×)

5. (3) 'Had' will be used in place of ' would have'. Read Explanation No.- 1.

6. (2) 'Had taken' will be used in place of 'has taken'. Since Principal Clause is in past tense. Therefore, the subordinate clause will also be in past tense. Here the Past Perfect Tense is suitable for the given sentence.

7. (2) 'Strikes' will be used in place of 'strike'.

8. (1) 'Has been' will be used in place of 'had been'.
   The Adjective- Immemorial means *beyond memory*, very old.

9. (2) 'Had' will be used in place of 'has'.

10. (3) 'Would have taken' will be used in place of 'would take'.

11. (3) 'Had been' will be used in place of 'was'.

12. (1) 'I have been suffering' will be used in place of 'I am suffering'.

13. (2) 'Had' will be used in place of 'has'.

14. (2) 'Has flowed' will be used in place of - 'has flown'. The verb -'fly' means 'to move through the air, using wings' and its past participle form is 'flown'.
    While the verb - 'flow' means 'to move steadily and continuously in one direction' (for liquid, gas, electricity) and its past participle form is flowed. There fore, 'Has flowed' is suitable for the meaning of the meaning of the given sentence.

15. (2) The verb - 'raise' will be used in place of the verb - 'rise'.
    The verb - 'rise' means ' to come or go upwards'; 'to reach a higher level or position'; 'to get up from a lying, sitting or kneeling position'; 'When the sun, moon etc rises, it appears above the horizon', While (= whereas) the verb - 'raise', means ' to lift or move something to a higher level', to move something/ somebody yourself to a vertical position', to increase the amount or level of something.

VOCABULARY

DETAILED SOLUTIONS

Q.1 *Find out the error part of the following sentences: (Article) (Noun) (Pronoun) (Adjective)*

1. The English (a) defeated (b) French (c) in the battle of water too (d) No error (e)

2. Never have I listened (a) to such a beautiful music (b)/as the piece we heard on radio (c)/ last night (d) No error (e)

3. The uncle of mine (a) / who is farmer (b) / gave me a piece of useful advice (c) when I went to see him three weeks ago (d)/ No error (e)

4. My neighbour along with his children (a)/ is going tonight (b)/ to see a Taj Mahal (c) at Agra (d) No error (e)

5. A first European (a) / sailor came to India (b) in modern times (c) was vasco-de-gama (d) No error (e)

6. Only a few girls (a) were above ground (b) the rest were (c) under the ground (d) No error (e)

7. Forty five students went (a) / to the church (b)/ yesterday to see/ (c) / the stained came home (d) / No error (e)

8. My elder sister came home (a) / after the sunset (b) / and had gone (c) / before sunrise (d) / No error (e)

9. Kabir and Rahim (a) / are great poets (b) / but the farmer is (c) / greater than later (d) / No error (e)

10. Mahatma Gandhi did not solve (a) / all the problems of the future (b) / but he did solve (c) / problems of his own age. (d) / No error (e)

11. Knowledge of regional language is (a) / necessary for bank officers because (b) / they are to understand (c) / what their customers say (d) / No error (e)

12. Child was looking out (a) / through the open window (b) / with fear (e) / in its eyes (d) / No error (e)

13. Everyone knows (a) / that leopard is (b) / faster then (c) / all other animals (d) / No error (c)

14. Have the trip to kashmir (a) / this autumn (b) / and weave (c) / romance in your life. (d) / No error (e)

15. Climbing the Mount Fuji (a) / in winter (b) / can be (c) / very dangerous (d) / No error (e)

16. There (a) / was (b) / a boy's college (c) / in my village (d) / No error (e)

17. Who (a) / has (b) / broken (c) the house's door (d) No error (e)

18. They (a) / were (b) / waiting for (c) / the train arrival (d) / No error (e)

19. Every teacher (a) / is expected (b) / to carry out (c) / his principal orders (d) / No error (e)

20. The climate (a) / of Ranchi (b) / is better (c) / than patna (d) / No error (e)

21. He (a) / is (b) a student of (c) / three year's degree course (d) / No error (e)

22. The life of the rich (a) / is (b) more luxurious than (c) / that of the poor's (d) / No error (e)

23. She told me (a) / that she had ever seen (b) / me with her (c) / mind's eyes (d) / No error (e)

24. The two friends (a) / pointed out (b) / each other merits and demerits (c) / before the teacher (d) / No error (e)

25. I don't think (a) / it is your house (b) / it is somebody's else (c) / No error

26. Mr shukla introduced (a) / to the principal (b) / as the monitor (c) / of the class (d) / No error (e)

27. This is a new book, but that is old ones

28. He must not do something for us.

29. She has bought a car, who is black

30. He is the dancer who we admire

31. A figure which four sides are equal is called a square

32. The dog who barked at him did not bite him.

33. We want to leave the house whom we rented last month.

ENGLISH

Correct the following sentences (adjective)

34. He saw two men, the one was lame and another was blind.
35. Shyama is more beautiful than any girl in the class.
36. My younger brother is six feet high.
37. The population of china is greater than India.
38. The students of Bihar are more laborious than Jharkhand.
39. Mrs Laloo Prasad Yadav is the most unique leader of India.
40. The girls were introduced to each other by a mutual friend.
41. If there were less cars on the roads, there would be less accidents.
42. I am looking forward to seeing you nearest sunday.
43. your essay is worst than mine.
44. I gave a few coins I had in my pocket to the beggar.
45. She got only passing marks in English.

Q.2 Fill in the blanks with suitable form of Adverbs and verb given in the brackets.

1. She works _____
   (a) hard   (b) hardly
   (c) harder   (d) hardness

2. I could _____ recognize her.
   (a) hard   (b) hardly
   (c) harder   (d) hardness

3. The teacher had come _____
   (a) just now   (b) justly
   (c) justify   (d) just

4. The boy was _____ asleep.
   (a) sound   (b) soundly
   (c) sound proof (d) sounded

5. He found the road _____
   (a) easy   (b) easily
   (c) easiest   (d) easier

6. Your _____ watch does not keep good time.
   (a) old   (b) older
   (c) oldest   (d) olded

7. Honey tastes _____
   (a) sweet   (b) sweeter
   (c) sweetest   (d) sweetful

8. The sky grew _____
   (a) dark   (b) darkest
   (c) darker   (d) darkfull

9. I gave her _____
   (a) punished   (b) punishment
   (c) punishable (d) punish

10. He is tired _____ poverty.
    (a) with   (b) of
    (c) for   (d) at

11. we were deprived _____ our freedom.
    (a) from   (b) of
    (c) for   (d) to

12. He enquired _____ the health.
    (a) after   (b) of
    (c) into   (d) about

13. The Indians fought _____ the English _____ freedom.
    (a) for; with (b) to; with
    (c) with ; for (d) to ; with

14. I differ _____ you.
    (a) from   (b) of
    (c) with   (d) for

15. India differs _____ England.
    (a) with   (b) from
    (c) of   (d) for

16. A father is blind _____ the faults of his son.
    (a) of   (b) to
    (c) with   (d) in

17. He is blessed _____ good health and is blessed _____ children.
    (a) with;in   (b) with ; into
    (c) in; with (d) of ; with

18. The responsibility is _____ my shoulders now.
    (a) at   (b) on
    (c) over   (d) off
19. The insects are a great nuisance_____ us.
    (a) with   (b) for
    (c) to   (d) at

Q.3 *Find out the error part of the following sentences : (Tense)*

1. I found this ring as I dig in the garden (a) / it looks very old (b) / I wonder whom it belongs to (c) / No error (d)
2. The girls were playing (a) / outside the house whereas (b) / the boys were sitting (c) / inside and played cards (d) / No error (e)
3. Mohini washes all her (a) / clothes and cooks food (b)/ for the family before (c) / she is going to the office (d) / No error (e)
4. I know nothing (a) / about chess because (b) / my game's teacher also (c) / was not knowing nothing about it (d) / No error (e)
5. He Happed to finish (a) / the work in the last week (b) / but in fact (c) / he could not (d) / No error (e)
6. He could not out (a) / the grass today because (b) / handle of the machine (c) / has broken a few days ago (d) / No error (e)
7. I have pleasure (a) / a certify (b) / that Shamim worked meritoriously (c) / for the last three years in our organization (d) / No error (e)
8. Yesterday Ramesh got (a)/ the information that his father (b) / died in an accident (c) / while travelling in a car. (d) / No error (e)
9. He will certainly help you (a) / if you will ask him (b) / in a pleasant manner (c) / No error (e)
10. He asked me (a) / if I am ill and (b) / I answered that I was not (c) / No error (d)

ENGLISH

Unit-3 READING COMPREHENSION

(A) FACTUAL PASSAGES

PASSAGE : 1

There are several indicators of a developed nation. It is economically, agriculturally and technologically advanced. There is all round prosperity. The benefits of prosperity reach the common people. They have a reasonable life span and enjoy the basic comforts and good health. They are able to educate and feed their children well. Poverty, illiteracy, ignorance, disease and inequalities are reduced to a minimum. Quality goods are produced in abundance and exports keep on rising. The nation is able to protect its security as it is self-reliant in defiance and has a standing in the international forum.

India, even after more than sixty five years since independence is branded as a developing country. Achieving the developed status means the major transformation of our national economy to make it one of the largest economies of the world, where people live well and above the poverty line. The transformation can be materialized within the next 15 to 20 years as India has the necessary potential. Our natural resources are richer as compared to those of many other countries. We have abundant supplies of all the ores and minerals. We have rich bio-diversity, abundant sunshine, varied agro-climatic conditions and plenty of rainfall all over India. The country either already has the necessary technologies or can develop them easily. Our people and our farmers not only have a great learning capability but most of them also have an entrepreneurial and competitive spirit. Avenues to channelise this spirit constructively and productively are required. We need the will to take-action and commit ourselves to be one of the world leaders. We must resolve to work hard with a long-term vision.

Technology is the highest wealth generator in the shortest possible time. It can provide us with infrastructure and help transform education and training, food and processing, industries and agriculture. It is the key to achieving quality products in an increasingly competitive market and to continually upgrading human skills. It is the only vital input for ensuring health security and better living conditions for people. It can enable us to double cereals by 2020 and to make-arrangements for their storage, transportation, distribution and marketing. It can make us leaders in machine tool industries. Through Software engineering we can enter computer-aided design and computer-aided manufacturing.

Therefore, the major role in India's development is to be played by the vast pool of our talented scientists, researchers and technologists. They should shed pessimism and think big because they are the only ones who understand the forces of technological modernisation. They should take is as a challenge to make India a developed country. They must spearhead the movement by talking about what can be done and encouraging people that difficulties can be overcome. They must extend all possible help to industries, business managers, administrators and others.

Questions:
(a) Write the basic fields in which a developed country is advanced.
(b) What kind of life do the people in a developed country live?
(c) What is required for achieving the developed status for India?
(d) "Technology is the highest wealth generator in the shortest time". How?
(e) Who can play a major role in India's development?
(f) How can India enter computer-aided design and manufacturing?

Find out a word from the passage which means:
(g) A machine for producing electricity = _____.
(h) A large quantity more than enough = _____.
(i) The state of having good fortune, wealth, money etc. _____.

FACTURAL PASSAGES

PASSAGE : 2

Prior to powering up the computer system, make sure that the power cord is firmly connected to the back panel of the CPU and is plugged into the wall socket.

Check if the video cable is firmly screwed to the port of the video cord with the other end connected to the back panel of the monitor.

Make sure that both the keyboard and mouse pointing device are securely plugged to the back panel. Also, check if they are connected to the correct port by checking on the markings.

When all connections are secure, start up the machine by pressing the power button normally located in the front panel of the CPU.

Depending on the configuration of the machine, a username and password may be requested; otherwise, the Operating System may be loaded directly to display the desktop to the user.

The proper way to turn off the computer system is by clicking on the 'start' button and choosing the 'Trun off Computer' option.

T adjust the monitor settings, right click on any blank portion of the desktop and select the 'Properties' option from the context menu.

On the 'Display Properties' window, select the 'Settings' tab to adjust the resolution of the screen.

For CD or DVD installers, insert the installation disk in the CD or DVD drive of the machine. This will be automatically read and launched by the Operating System.

To extend the functionality of any computer system. Software is normally installed into the local hard drive. A software installer may be through some media like a CD or DVD or from being downloaded from the Internet.

When the installation process is initiated, a new window will normally be displayed to the used. Majority of newer installers provide either a default or an advanced installation procedure. In most cases, simply click on the default process to allow the installer to complete the entire process with minimum user intervention. Upon completion of the installation process, a user may be prompted to reboot the machine.

To launch the software, simply click on the 'Start' Menu, choose 'All Programs' and select from the menu the program intended to be run. An alternative to this process is to check if a shortcut link is created on the Desktop. Clicking this icon will also launch the associated program.

Questions :

(i) Where is the power cord connected?
(ii) What are securely plugged to the back panel?
(iii) When is new machine started up?
(iv) 'The proper way to turn off the computer system is.....' How?
(v) Why do you right click on any blank portion of the desktop?
(vi) How is the software launched?

Find out a word from the passage which means:

(vii) one part of something larger
(viii) a list of possible choices shown on a computer screen
(ix) a think you can choose out of two or more possibilities

ENGLISH

PASSAGE : 3

The seasonal problem of water taps running dry is plaguing most of our major cities. With the bigger rivers flowing in trickles and ponds and wells reduced to claypits, village women in remote areas have to fetch every drop of water for drinking, cooking, washing and so on, across large distances. This has only worsened a perennial problem, that of widespread pollution of water, rendering it unfit for human consumption. The monsoons-and the attendant floods - will not solve this problem. The Delhi Administration is seriously worried about the threat to civic health posed by the polluted waters of the Jamuna. Two new tanks are to be set up to treat sewage. At present only 60 per cent of the 200 million gallons of the city's sewage receives any kind of treatment before it is dumped into the river which supplies water not only to this city but to innumerable towns and villages downstream. The Ganga, the Jamuna, the Cauvery, in fact all our important rivers, serving many urban conglomerations are fast becoming a major source of disease.

A comprehensive bill, introduced in Parliament recently, envisages the setting up of Central and State boards for the prevention and control of water pollution. But is will obviously take some time before legislation is passed and effectively implemented. Meanwhile the problem continues to swell.

According to a survey of eight developing countries conducted a couple of years ago, 90 per cent of all child deaths were due to water-borne diseases. It is the same unchanged story today. In a country like India, a burgeoning population continuing to use the open countryside as a lavatory means that, with every dust storm and rain, human excreta laden with germs and parasite spores find their way to ponds, shallow wells and even the streams and rivers. Only 18 per cent of the rural folk have access to potable water.

A new threat that has already assumed alarming proportions is from industrial waste which is generally dumped, untreated, into the nearest river. For instance, for every kilogram of processed hide, 30-40 litres of foul smelling waste water has to be disposed of. There are at least 900 licensed tanneries in the organized sector. Putrefied paper and jute waste, metallic waste from straw board and textile mills, sulphur, ammonia, urea, metallic salts and corrosive acids - all find their way to the rivers of India.

It is important not only to make new laws to ensure the purity of water, but also to realize the urgency of implementing them ruthlessly, if we are to avoid a national health disaster cutting across the barrir between towns and the countryside.

Questions :

(i) Which seasonal problem plagues our major cities?
(ii) How has water pollution become a health hazard?
(iii) What does the bill introduced in Parliament envisage?
(iv) What has the survey of developing countries revealed?
(v) How is human excreta a major source of disease in India?
(vi) Which new threat is the writer talking about?

Find out a word from the passage which means:

(vii) countless
(viii) complete
(ix) cruelly

FACTUAL PASSAGES

PASSAGE : 4 (Discursive)

Health is a positive state of physical and mental well-being. When we feel secure-by being physical y healthy and free from disease, by feeling contact, and by living in a comfortable and clean environment......we are in a state of positive health Our close and harmonious interactions with family members, neighbors, and friends help us stay well mentally.

According to this definition, very few people in the world enjoy positive health. In the rich and developed countries, family ties appear to be weakening, neighbor's may be stranger and friendship is sometime restricted to business contacts. In those countries environmental conditions have improved considerably. The populations have achieved a better nutritional status, and there is often plenty of money available to buy most of life's comfort. People in developed countries may enjoy better physical health, but they are far from achieving positive health, as many are not so contented. On the other hand, in the developing counties, the quality of human interactions within families, neighbor and friend are often more positive. However, both the environmental and nutritional status of these populations are lower, o the people suffer more from poor physical health. When a person's physical health i poor, the state of positive health cannot exist. So, we find that positive health is eluding many of us.

However, it is not impossible for people in developing countries to achieve positive health. To help achieve this state, we need an understanding of how our bodies function so that we can keep healthy; we also need a clean environment and healthy food that doe not cost too much money. We need proper education for all people that leads to understanding the relationship between health and a positive approach to life.

(a) On the basis of your reading of the above passage make note on it, using heading and subheading.
(b) Write a summary of the passage and suggest a suitable title.

PASSAGE : 5 (Literary)

There are seven schools of Yoga, differing from one another, and yet having a common objective. The system expounded by Patanjali in his 'Yoga Sutras' is that of Raja Yoga and includes much of the teaching of the other six. 'Hatha Yoga' consists largely of a system of bodily exercises calculated to stimulate the mental and spiritual faculties. 'Mantra Yoga' is a ritualistic course of mediation on certain mystical syllables 'Bhakti Yoga' emphasizes devotion. The remaining school do not command much importance.

It may be worthwhile examining if the yoga method and the modern technique of Mental Hygiene have any common features. Yoga in the words of Patanjali "is attained by studying the fluctuation of the mind".

The student of yoga is necessarily one who is dissatisfied with his own adaptation to life and to the external world, for no other reason would induce a man to engage in such an exacting course. His search is not avowedly a search for God, but rather a striving for self-knowledge and internal mental balance. Patanjali says that if the student is of such a temperament that the idea of God appeals to him. that is to be encouraged, for the approach to equilibrium through devotion to God is thereby made the more rapid. If, on the other had, the student is unable to accept the hypothesis of God, there are other path of approach. Yoga, in other words, encourages but does not insist upon the devotional approach. Even though Mental Hygiene is intimately associated with Ethics and Religion and the study must confine itself to the psychological aspects of the subject.

(a) On the basis of your reading of the above passage make note on it, using heading and subheading.
(b) Write a summary of the passage and suggest a suitable title.

ENGLISH

(B) DICUERSIVE PASSAGES

PASSAGE : 1

Egotism is the most common fault of mankind. Product of the perfectly natural desire to display oneself, egotism, which is an exaggerated form of self-display, can take such a variety of shapes that it is not always easy to discern. Beyond any shadow of doubt, however, it is a personal defect that ought to be constantly hunted down and scotched, for it impairs the personality, and frustrates all efforts at self-improvement.

This is the easily recognizable form of egotism that is evidenced in the person who continually talks of his own affairs. You must all have met the kind of man who is never happy when recounting his exploits and experiences in life; and whatever subject he may begin discussing you fell quite sure that he will sooner or later arrive at himself. Although such a blatant kind of egotism is apparent to the onlooker, it may not be so easy for the egotist himself to recognize his fault. But if he can put on his guard-and it behaves each one of us to examine carefully whether we are entirely immune from this canker-there is always hope of a cure. On the other hand, there is a type, not uncommon, which evidences its egotism by affecting a humility that is certainly not felt, and ostentatiously avoiding the use of the pronoun"I" in speech and in writing. Such affectation is an infallible sign of egotism, and it is all the more reprehensible because it is deliberately assumed by the person.

Next we come to the individual who holds strong opinions and insists on forcing these opinions onto others. He constantly lays down the law, he knows and he jolly well insists that you shall accept his viewpoints. Here again, there is not a great difficulty in recognizing the egotistical aspect of this conduct, although it is not so easy to remove such a defect, for a person of this kind is generally possessed of a fiery temper-but again, it can be done, and recognition of the defect is the first step towards its cure.

There are two other well-known types of egotists- the over-precise person and the officious one. The former offends by his meticulous habits, his insistence on having everything just right -just right generally connoting the way he personally wants them to be. The officious individual succeeds in making himself most disliked because of his detestable habit of always showing or telling other people how to do things. He will glibly appeal to duty; he will continually find fault with another's way of doing things, and point out the immense superiority of his method. In his own eyes, he is always right.

Questions:

(i) What is egotism?

(ii) Why should egotism be scotched?

(iii) Which is the easily recognizable form of egotism?

(iv) Which affectation is an infallible sign of egotism?

(v) How does an over-precise person offend others?

(vi) Why is an officious person most disliked?

Find out a word from the passage which means:

(vii) damages (something)

(viii) showing strong emotions

(ix) on purpose/intentionally

FACTUAL PASSAGES

PASSAGE : 2

Success comes to those who work with concentration and have thoroughness in action. Anyone who achieves success in the management of any great affair of life is entitled to honor. May he be an artist who paints a picture, an author who writes a book, a housewife who manages the household affairs or a soldier who wins the battle-the credit goes to his ardent spirit which is responsible for getting the job done thoroughly without getting discouraged by the failure. Nothing great and durable was ever achieved without perseverance. It is only by practice, patience, labour, thoroughness and an eye for perfection that man reaches the minutest detail of the problem, overcomes them and attains his goal. There is not even a single statesman who has not been a man of industry. Louis XIV rightly said, "It is by toil that kings govern". Washington, an indefatigable man of business trained himself in the habits of application, study and methodical work and successfully brought to bear in the affairs of the government. Wellington, the head of his army in Spain directed the precise manner in which the soldiers were to cook their breakfast while on duty. He specified the exact speed at which bullocks were to be driven. If every detail in equipment is carefully arranged and well executed, then efficiency is secured.

Booker T. Washington, a great racial American leader and educator gained admission to the Hampton Normal and Agricultural Institute, Virginia when the head teacher got impressed by the quality of thoroughness in work. When asked to clean the adjoining room, he swept the room three times and dusted every bit of furniture four times. This superb quality of thoroughness in work. When asked to clean the adjoining room, he swept the room three times and dusted every bit of furniture four times. This superb quality of thoroughness in work impressed the head teacher and Washington got admission in the school of his dreams.

So it should be borne in mind that behind every dream and success lies a long trail of passionate efforts which the world may never come to know. But if anyone thinks that great success can be achieved without thoroughness, then it is better if thoroughness becomes our second nature and with the boon bestowed upon us, we can reap the harvest of our toil for the rest of our lives.

(a) **On the basis of your reading of the above passage make note on it, using heading and subheading.**
(b) **Write a summary of the passage and suggest a suitable title.**

PASSAGE : 3 (Discursive)

Modern life is sophisticated and complex. Simple living and high thinking is a thing of the past. Complex living and low thinking has replaced this motto. Most of the people are artificial and sophisticated. They have one thing in their heart and another on their lips. Majority of the people in the cities are deceitful. Face is no more the index of mind. Only expert psychologists can study the character of a man from the outlook of a person. The world is full of cheats and robbers. Many a man with simple looks may be a crook in reality. It is a world of make belief and show business. Acting and mannerism are the rule of the day. The new generation is clear and smart. It is beyond recognition. Very few people are dependable in respect of their character and integrity.

ENGLISH

In this world of complexity and artificiality, manners are all important. You cannot move in society unless you know about good manners and possess them. Even if you may not have good meals, you have to maintain certain minimum standards of dress and make-up. Manners have become a part and parcel of life. Without proper manners you are not welcome anywhere. However honest may be your intention and however innocent your behaviour, unless you can put up tactful show of manners, you will not earn respect of your fellow beings.

For good manners you must maintain a good personality. A clean dress, a clean body, well brushed hair, style of dress in keeping with the times, a good power of speech and conversation, a certain patience in giving ears to the other party are necessary qualifications of a person professing to know manners. These qualifications are important for success in may walk of life. Their importance is all pervading in modern times. Simplicity, innocence, honesty and similar traits of this kind have lost their values. These traits make a simpleton of any intelligent person in modern society.

(a) **On the basis of your reading of the above passage make note on it, using heading and subheading.**
(b) **Write a summary of the passage and suggest a suitable title.**

PASSAGE : 4

Effective speaking depends on effective listening. It takes energy to concentrate on hearing and to concentrate on understanding what has been heard. Incompetent listeners fail in a number of ways. First, they may drift. Their attention drifts from what the speaker is saying. Second, they may counter. They find counter arguments to whatever a speaker may be saying. Third, they compete. Then they filter. They exclude from their understanding those parts of the message which do not readily fit with their own frame of reference. Finally they react. They let personal feelings about speaker or subject override the significance of the message which is being sent.

What can a listener do to be more effective? The first key to effective listening is the art of concentration. IF a listener positively wishes to concentrate on receiving a message then his chances of success are high.

It may need determination. Some speakers are difficult to follow. either because of voice problems, or because of the form in which they send a message. There is then a particular need for the determination of a listener to concentrate on what is being said.

Concentration is helped by alertness. Mental alertness is helped by physical alertness. It is not simply physical fitness, but positioning of the body, the limbs and the side. One useful way for achieving concentration is intensive note-taking, by trying to capture the important points the speaker is referring to. Note-taking has been recommended as an aid to the listener. It helps the speaker too. It gives him confidence when he sees that listeners are sufficiently interested to take notes; the patterns of eye-contact with the listener can be very positive. The speaker also make effective use of pauses.

Posture too is important. Consider the impact made by a less competent listener who pushes his chair backwards and slouches. An upright posture helps a listener's concentration. At the same time it is seen by the speaker to be a positive feature amongst his listeners. Effective listening skills have an impact on both the listener and the speaker.

(a) **On the basis of your reading of the above passage make note on it, using heading and subheading.**
(b) **Write a summary of the passage and suggest a suitable title.**

FACTUAL PASSAGES

PASSAGE : 5

Everyone needs a holiday, both to relax and to have a change of environment. The holiday makers feel relaxed and refreshed at the end of the holiday and look forward to the resumption of their duties, be it at school, office or factories, with renewed vigor. This is the reason why all establishments grant their employees annual leave. With the end of the Academic year the schools and universities grant their pupils a long holiday during mid-summer. This will last until early September when the new school term starts. Of course the parents will like to take advantage of this and take their leave to coincide with the children's vacation. This has become a traditional holiday season in most European countries particularly in England. With the coming of August, the traditional holiday season in Britain reaches its peak point and most of the holiday resorts are packed to capacity. In order to avoid the crowd, some prefer to take their holiday a little earlier if facilities so warrant. Those who have already taken their holidays can console themselves not only with reflections on the happy days spent in the country, at the seaside or abroad, but also with the thought that holiday expenses are over for the year and that by taking an earlier holiday they have missed the August rush.

The main thing, of course, is the weather and that it would be hazardous to prophesy. But whatever the weather is like, the essence of a holiday for most is the worries behind" is the sound advice for the holiday maker. Private worries are not always easy to escape from. However, even the pessimist would admit that for the moment things appear brighter than they have been.

Holiday time is surely a time for shedding serious preoccupations and seeking the pleasures that appeal to us. It is true that we may not always succeed in finding them, indeed there are people who maintain that the great thing about a holiday is that it gives you an ampler appreciation of home comforts.- a view no doubt more widely held among the elderly than you.

(a) On the basis of your reading of the above passage make note on it, using heading and subheading.
(b) Write a summary of the passage and suggest a suitable title.

PASSAGE : 6

EVERY friend saith "I am his friend"; but there is a friend, which is only a friend in name. Is it not a grief even unto death, when a companion and friend is turned to an enemy? O wicked imagination, wherefore waste thou created -to fill the face of the earth with deceit? Base is the friend who hath regard to one's table, but in time of affliction standees aloof. A good friend contended with one's enemy, and taketh hold of the shield against the adversary.

Every counsellor extolled his own counsel, but there is that counselled a way to suit himself. Let thy soul beware of such a counsellor and inform thyself of him beforehand, for he himself will also take thought why matters should fall out as he wished, and will say into thee, "Thy way is good" and then stand off to watch thy misfortune. Take not counsel with one that looked askance at three; and hide thy counsel from such as are jealous of thee. Consult not with a woman touching her of whom she is jealous, neither with a coward about was; nor with a merchant about exchange; nor with a buyer about selling; nor with a niggard about benevolence; nor with an unmerciful man about kindliness; nor with a sluggard about any kind of work; nor with the yearly hireling concerning seed time; nor with an idle servant about much business: give not heed to these in any matter of counsel, but rather be continually with a godly man, whom thou shalt have known to be a keeper of the commandments, whose heart is at one with thine own and who, if thou stumble, will be grieved for thee.

And let the counsel of thine own heart stand, for there is none more faithful unto thee than it.

(a) On the basis of your reading of the above passage make note on it, using heading and subheading.
(b) Write a summary of the passage and suggest a suitable title.

ENGLISH

PASSAGE : 7

Swami Vivekananda was born in an aristocratic Bengali Kayastha family of Calcutta on January 12, 1863. Vivekananda's parents influenced his thinking - his father by his rationality and his mother by her religious temperament. From his childhood, he showed an inclination towards spirituality and God realization. His guru, Ramakrishna, taught him Advaita Vedanta (non-dualism); that all religions are true and that service to man was the most effective worship of God. After the death of his Guru, Vivekananda became a wandering monk, touring the Indian subcontinent and acquiring first-hand knowledge of conditions in India. A spiritual genius of commanding intellect and power, Vivekananda crammed immense labour and achievement into his short life. The youthful Vivekananda embraced the agnostic philosophies of the Western mind along with the worship of science.

At the same time, vehement in his desire to know the truth about God, he questioned people of holy reputation, asking them if they had seen God. He found such a person in Sri Ramakrishna, who became his master, allayed his doubts, gave him God vision, and transformed him into sage and prophet with authority to teach.

After Sri Ramakrishna's death, Vivekananda renounced the world and criss-crossed India. His mounting compassion for India's people drove him to seek their material help from the West. Accepting an opportunity to represent Hinduism at Chicago's Parliament of Religions in 18983, Vivekananda won instant celebrity in America and a ready forum for his spiritual teaching.

For three years he spread the Vedanta philosophy and religion in America and England and then returned to India to found the Ramakrishna Math and Mission. Exhorting his nation to spiritual greatness, he wakened India to a new national consciousness. He died July 4, 1902, after a second, much shorter sojourn in the West. His lectures and writings have been gathered into nine volumes.

(a) On the basis of your reading of the above passage make note on it, using heading and subheading.

(b) Write a summary of the passage and suggest a suitable title.

ANSWER TO PASSAGE :

(a) **NOTES :**

False Friends And True Friends

(A) FALSE FRIEND

    (i) Regards one's table but stands alone in need

(B) TRUE FRIEND

    (i) Shield against the adversary

(C) TAKE NOT COUNSEL FROM

(i) That counselled a way to suit himself

(ii) That wishes to watch thy misfortune

(iii) That has jealousy

(iv) A coward about war, merchant about exchange, buyer about selling, niggard about benevolence, unmerciful man about kindliness, sluggard about work.

(D) TAKE COUNSEL FROM

(i) A Godly man

(ii) He who grieves when you stumble

(iii) Of thine own heart

FACTURAL PASSAGES

(b) **SUMMARY :**

Title : False Friends And True Friends

Friends can be false or true. A false friend regards one's table but stands alone in need. A true friend always shields you against the adversary. In life you shouldn't take counsel from a man who counsels a way to suit himself, or who wishes to watch your misfortune or who has jealousy of you. Never take counsel from a coward about war, merchant about exchange, buyer about selling, niggard about benevolence, unmerciful man about kindness and sluggard about work. Always take counsel from a Godly man or he who grieves when you stumble or your own heart.

Answer to Passage :

(a) **NOTES :**

Swami Vivekananda

(A) BIRTH, PARENTAGE, TEMPERAMENT

(i) Born in an aristocratic Bengali Kayastha family of Calcutta on 12 Jan. 1863
(ii) Rational father, religious mother
(iii) Inclination towards spirituality

(B) JOINED A GURU, UNDERTOOK TOUR

(i) Joined Guru Ramkrishna Paramhansa
(ii) Undertook tour of India.

(C) ATTENDED CHICAGO'S PARLIAMENT OF RELIGIONS 1893

(i) Instant celebrity in America
(ii) Spread Vedanta Philosophy in US, UK for three years

(D) DEATH

(i) 4 July 1902

(b) **SUMMARY :**

Title : Swami Vivekananda

Swami Vivekananda was born in an aristocratic Bengali Kayastha family of Calcutta on 12 Jan. 1863. He had rational father and religious mother. He had inclination towards spirituality. He joined Guru Ramkrishna Paramhansa. He taught him non-dualism and God realization. After the death of his Guru he undertook the tour of India. He got first had an experience. In 1893 he attended Chicago's Parliament of Religions. He became an instant celebrity in America For three years he spread Vedanta Philosophy in US and UK. He died on 4 July 1902.

PASSAGE : 8

1. Read the following passage carefully.

1. One of the great values of punctuality is that is that it gives discipline to life. We have to get up in time. We have to do things at the appointed time. All these entail certain amount of sacrifice. It dispels laziness and removes over 'take-it-easy attitude'. A disciplined person always gets recognition and social acceptance. He is wanted and appreciated. Therefore, punctuality can make us socially acceptable people.

2. Another significant merit of punctuality is that it provides ample time to do our work correctly and properly. Doing things hurriedly or haphazardly can have disastrous consequences. When we do things in time there is every chance that they end up as fine works.

3. The virtue of punctuality is said to be the key to success. Look at the great world leaders who has achieved fame and success. Punctuality was their hallmark. They kept their promises. Punctuality is a virtue that is appreciated by all. Washington once took his secretary to task for being late. The secretary laid the blame upon his watch. Washington reported: "Then, Sir either you must get a new watch or I must get a new secretary." People like them are ideals whom we should follow in earnest.

ENGLISH

4. When individuals are not punctual they cause a lot of inconvenience to others. People have to wait for them and waste their valueable time. Want of punchuality reveals want of culture and is discourteous to the person we fail.

   Unpunctuality invites trouble and worry. History is full of cases which show that lack of punctuality has caused defeat, loss of kingdom and golden opportunities. It is said that Napoleon lost the battle of Waterloo in 1815 because one of his generals came late. Many people lose good opportunities of job or promotion when they reach late for appointment.

5. All of us are notborn with the virtue of punctuality. We have to cultivate it painstakingly. Only constant vigil and practice can implant this virtue.

   It calls for great deal of sacrifice. It calls for courage to root out laziness and the 'take-it-easy attitude'. It demands a disciplined life. That is why very few individuals have the virtue of punctuality. But, know it for certain that it is the surest way to success.

On the basis of your understanding of the passage attempt the following questions.

(a) **What do you mean by the great value of punctuality?**
   (i) It entails certain amount of sacrifices.
   (ii) It helps in getting up in time.
   (iii) It gives discipline to life.
   (iv) It dispels laziness.

Ans. (iii) It gives discipline to life.

(b) **Choose the option that best matches with word 'punctuality' as used in the passage.**
   (i) Another significant merit of punctuality is that it provides ample time to do our work correctly and properly.
   (ii) Another significant merit of laziness is that it provides ample time to do our work correctly and properly.
   (iii) Another significant merit of entertainment is that it provides ample time to do our work correctly and properly.
   (iv) Another significant merit of time is that it provides ample time to do our work correctly and properly.

Ans. (i) Another significant merit of punctuality is that it provides ample time to do our work correctly and properly.

(c) **Choose the option that completes the sentence given below.**
   The...............of punctuality is said to be the key to ....
   1. virtue   2. merit   3. failure   4. inconvenience
   5. success
   (i) 2 and 3   (ii) 1 and 5   (iii) 3 and 4   (iv) 2 and 4

Ans. (ii) 1 and 5

(d) **What do individuals do when they are not punctual?**
   (i) They cause a let of inconvenience to others.
   (ii) They cause a let of conveniences to others.
   (iii) They invite trouble and worry.
   (iv) They keep their promises.

Ans. (i) They cause a let of inconvenience to others.

(e) **What does the want of punctuality reveal ?**
   (i) Want of entertainment   (ii) Want of study
   (iii) Want of civilization   (iv) What of culture

Ans. (iii) Want of civilization

FACTURAL PASSAGES

(f) Which battle did Napoleon lose and why?

1. Battle of Panipat
2. Battle of Waterloo
3. One of his generals came late
4. He entertained whole night.
5. He was badly tired.

(i) 2 and 3 (ii) 1 and 4 (iii) 1 and 5 (iv) 2 and 5

Ans. (ii) 2 and 3

(g) Choose the option that vest matches with the word 'virtue' as used in the passage.

(i) Only constant vigil and practice can implant failure.
(ii) Only constant vigil and practice can implant virtue.
(iii) Only constant vigil and practice can implant success.
(iv) Only constant vigil and practice can implant tiredness.

Ans. (ii) Only constant vigil and practice can implant virtue.

(h) Choose the option that completes the following sentence.

It calls for .... to root out .... and the 'take-it-easy attitude'.

1. afraid 2. bravery 3. entertainment 4. courage
5. laziness

(i) 1 and 2 (ii) 3 and 4 (iii) 4 and 5 (iv) 1 and 5

Ans. (iii) 4 and 5

(i) Choose the option that completes the following sentence.

History is full of cases which show that.............. has caused defeat, ... and........ .

1. lack of punctuality 2. paucity of water 3. less of kingdom 4. reaching late for appointment
5. golden opportunities

(i) 1, 3 and 5 (ii) 1, 2 and 4 (iii) 2, 3 and 4 (iv) 1, 2 and 5

Ans. (i) 1, 3 and 5

(j) Who once took his secretary to task for being late?

(i) Churchill (ii) Napoleon (iii) Washington (iv) George Bush

Ans. (iii) Washington

PASSAGE : 9

2. Read the following passage carefully.

1. With the next round of the Commonwealth Games coming up this year, sports fans are already speculating about the likely winners from India. While chances appear bright in some sporting activities, in others the picture appears dismal. Chances of India throwing up a few surprises is always discussed among sports lovers. Most game watchers predict that while India can add more to its medals tally in the shooting events, the chances of improving her status in the swimming category appear slim, despite the potential of creating good swimmers in this country.

2. One sport in the country with tremendous potential but pathetic performance is swimming. The country is flooded with talented swimmers and coaches whose potential is not fully utilised due to red-tapes' and bureaucratic hurdles. In spite of being a country full of rivers and canals, swimming has failed to capture the imagination of Indians at large. The Government, on its part, has done very little to boost the sport.

ENGLISH

3. All those persons, who are interested in swimming, realise that bad quality of water is one rampant problem with almost 90% of swimming pools. As for schools, it requires exorbitant sums of money and the schools cannot afford it. A handful of the privileged few, who enjoy this luxury, fall in the category of the elite. These are out of reach of the common man.

4. Where do the Indians stand today in comparison with international swimmers? The history of swimming in India has not been too bright. International winners have excellent facilities in terms of coaching, nuitrition, tactics, positive attitude and hard work. Paucity of high caliber international coaches is one setback Indians have suffered in all the arenas of sport. Thanks to the petty gains and trivial politics, the good ones are dropped like a hot potato and the blue-eyes ones taken over for participating in international matches. Except for the metros, the country is deprived of good Olympic-size swimming pools.

5. The government and sports organisations will have to make serious efforts to transform the future of Indian sports. Till then, it is a long, long wait.

On the basis of your understanding of the passage attempt the following questions.

(a) Which word from the passage matches best with the word 'contemplating'
   (i) coming   (ii) winning   (iii) speculating   (iv) watching
Ans. (iii) speculating

(b) Which word from the passage matches best with the word 'astonishes'?
   (i) surprises   (ii) chances
   (iii) categories   (iv) suffers
Ans. (i) surprises

(c) What has been the history of swimming in India?
   (i) wonderful   (ii) natural   (iii) very bright   (iv) not too bright
Ans. (iv) not to bright

(d) What would be the synonym of the word 'prospective'?
   (i) pathetic   (ii) privileged   (iii) potential   (iv) paucity
Ans. (iii) potential

(e) What would be the synonym of the word 'massive'?
   (i) flooded   (ii) Tremendous   (iii) hurdles   (iv) capture
Ans. (ii) Tremendous

(f) What would be the antonym of the word 'unpopular'?
   (i) portrait   (ii) photograph   (iii) project   (iv) favorite
Ans. (iv) favorite

(g) What kind of efforts do the government and sports organisations need to make to transform the future of Indian sports?
   (i) comparative efforts   (ii) Trivial Efforts
   (iii) Non-serious efforts   (iv) Serious efforts
Ans. (iv) serious efforts

FACTURAL PASSAGES

(h) Choose the correct option to fill in the blank in the given sentence.

As for............, it requires................sums of money and the schools cannot afford it.

1. hospitals   2. institutes   3. schools   4. companies
5. exorbitant

(i) 3 and 5   (ii) 1 and 4   (iii) 2 and 3   (iv) 1 and 5

Ans. (i) 3 and 5

(i) Choose the correct option to fill in the blanks in the sentence given below.

Paucity of high ....international coaches is one setback..............have suffered in all the arenas of sports.

1. powerful   2. caliber   3. Americans   4. Indians
5. Russians

(i) 1 and 5   (ii) 2 and 4   (iii) 2 and 3   (iv) 3 and 4

Ans. (i) 2 and 4

(j) Choose the correct option given below to fill in the blanks.

Most game ....predict that while India can add more to its medal tally in the............... events.

1. audiences   2. watchers   3. shooting   4. archery
5. hockey

(i) 2 and 3   (ii) 1 and 3   (iii) 1 and 4   (iv) 2 and 5

Ans. (i) 2 and 3

PASSAGE : 10

3. Read the following passage carefully.

1. Certain foods can rejuvenate and activate the body, inducing even stable mental health and the advisory positions about the remarkable healing power of food. To recognise, isolate and increase the intake of foods that have large amounts of disease fighting antioxidants, to identify the two kinds of fat; the beneficial Omega-3 and the Omega-6, in which foods are commonly cooked; to alienate allergies caused by foods that work against the human metabolism.

2. Ever oxygen has certain toxic forms called oxides, which spark off lethal reactions that have been linked to sixty odd chronic diseases, one of which is ageing, Antioxidants minimise the effects of the oxidants. Plant foods, thankfully are packed with antioxidant agents. Scientists are now researching into an antioxidant "Status report" based on individual blood tests; if the antioxidants are funning low, specific food should be prescribed to boost the levels.

3. Fat comes in two types - Omega-3 which is found in marine life and Omega-6 which is concentrated in vegetable oils. The first is good, the other is plain rotten.

4. The best source of Omega-3 is preferably sea fish. But frying it in Omega-6 rich vegetable oil kills all its goodness. The third imperative in codifying food health is through identifying irritants.

5. While some foods cause obvious and easily identified allergies like rashes, others cause either delayed reactions or minor irritants which could, nonetheless, be a serious deterrent to general well-being. Obstinate amoebiasis, nagging depression and persistent headaches are the most obvious symptoms. Food plays a dramatic role in alerting and fine-tuning of brain cells to give them sharper concentration. An innocuous combination of red wine and cheese can trigger off migraine.

ENGLISH

6. Ageing brains have low levels of thiamin, which is concentrated in wheat-germ and bran, nuts, meat and cereals. More good brain-food comes from liver, milk and almonds, which are rich in riboflavin and extremely good for memory. Carotene, available in deep green leafy vegetables and fruits, is also good for geriatric brains. So is a high iron diet: it can make old brains gallop hyperactively like young ones. Iron comes from greens; liver, shell-fish, red meat and soyabeans. Sea-food, very high in iron, is an excellent diet supplement.

7. The New England Journal of Medicine reported in its May 1985 issue that 30 grams of fish a day could result in a dramatic drop in the chances of acquiring a cardiovascular disease.

3.1 Read the given questions and write the answer in about 30-40 words:

(a) **What are oxides? What effect do they have on the human body?**

Ans. Certain toxic forms of oxygen are known as oxides. Oxides spark off lethal reaction in the body and have been linked to around 60 chronic diseases, including the process of ageing.

(b) **Why are antioxidants necessary? Which foods are rich in antioxidants?**

Ans. Antioxidants are useful in fighting diseases and minimising the effects of oxidants. Plant foods and other specific foods that are rich in antioxidant agents are prescribed for boosting antioxidant levels in humans. These are prescribed following individual blood tests.

(c) **Where is Omega-3 found? How can the good effect of Omega-3 fats be killed by Omega-6 fats?**

Ans. Omega-3 fats are found in marine life, particularly in sea fish. The positive properties of Omega-3 fat get nullified when the fish is fried in vegetable oils containing Omega-6.

(d) **What foods are necessary for geriatric brains?**

Ans. Foods with concentrated levels of thiamine, such as wheat-germ, and bran, nuts, meat and cereals, are good for geriatric brains. Also liver, milk, almonds, carotene-rich foods, fruits and an overall high iron diet are good for geriatric brains.

3.2 On the basis of your reading of the passage, answer the following:

(a) **A harmless combination of red wine and cheese can trigger off:**

　　(i) bodyache　　(ii) nausea　　(iii) cough and sneezing　　(iv) headache

Ans. (iv) headache

(b) **Iron comes from:**

　　(i) liver and shell-fish　　(ii) greens
　　(iii) sea food and red meat　　(iv) all of the above

Ans. (iv) all of the above

(c) **Fat comes in two types Omega-3 and ....**

Ans. Omega -6

(d) **Write the antonym of the word 'marked'. (para 5)**

Ans. 'innocuous'

FACTUAL PASSAGES

(C) LITERARY PASSAGES

PASSAGE : 1

In 1567, when Crown Prince Pratap Singh was only 27, Chittor was surrounded by the Mughal forces of Emperor Akbar. Maharana Udai Singh II decided to leave Chittor and move his family to Gogunda, rather than capitulate to the Mughals. The young Pratap Singh wanted to stay back and fight the Mughals but the elders intervened and convinced him to leave Chittor, oblivious of the fact that this move from Chittor was going to create a history for all times to come.

Maharana Pratap was born on May 9th 1540 in Kumbhalgarh, Rajasthan. His father was Maharana Udai Singh II and his mother was Rani Jeevant Kanwar Maharana Udia Singh II ruled the kingdom of Mewar, with his capital at Chittor. Maharana Pratap was the eldest of twenty-five sons and hence given the title of Crown Prince. He was destined to be the 54th ruler of Mewar, in the line of the Sisodiya Rajputs.

Rana Pratap took a vow to get back Chittor. A great battle was fought at Haldighti. The great Mughal army under the command of famous general Man Singh and Prince Salim fought Rana with his brave soldiers. Rana and his soldiers fought bravely but suffered heavy loss. And he with his family had to retire in the jungle. They had almost nothing to eat. One day a cat took away the only loaf from the princess's hand. She began to weep. The sight moved the brave heart of Rana. He wept like a child.

Now he decided to send a letter to Akbar and to surrender before him. But just then his old and faithful minister, Bhama Shah came to him and placed all his wealth at his feet to get an army and fight with Akbar. The Rana accepted the offer and made an army. He captured many places but could not get back Chittor.

So, Rana made a vow not to sleep on the bed and under a roof till he got back to Chittor. So his descendants honour his name and vow even putting some Khusa grass under their beds. There is a class of Rajputs who still lead a wonderful life. They recently entered the city of Chittor under the command of Jawahar Lal Nehru with great pomp and ceremony to settle and live there in the free India.

India is proud of Rana Pratap who never bowed his head before the mighty Akbar, the Emperor. He suffered hardships with patience but never yielded to the force of Akbar. He was a true patriot.

Questions:

(i) Who was the king of Mewar in 1567?
(ii) What do you know about the birth of Maharana Pratap?
(iii) Why was prince Pratap Singh given the title of Crown Prince?
(iv) Where was the great battle fought?
(v) Who helped Rana to raise army again?
(vi) Why is India proud of Maharana Pratap?

Find out a word from the passage which means:

(vii) not aware of something
(viii) a formal and serious promise
(ix) surrendered before somebody/something

ENGLISH

PASSAGE : 2

Candida - Never mind that just at present. Now I want you to look at this other boy here. my born was spoiled by love of his parents since his birth. We go once a fortnight to see his parents. You should come with us, Eugene, to see the pictures of the hero of that family. James as a baby, the most wonderful of all babies. James holding his first school prize, won at the ripe age of eight; James as the captain of his college cricket team; James in his first frock coat. James under all sorts of glorious circumstances. You know how strong he is (1 hope he didn't hurt you) : how clever he is : how happy (with increasing seriousness). Ask James's mother and his three sisters what it cost them to save James the trouble of doing anything except being strong, clever and happy. Ask me what trouble it costs me to be James' mother and three sisters, and wife, and mother to his children, all in one. Ask Prosy and Maria how troublesome the house is even when we have no visitors to help us slice the onions. Ask the tradesmen who want to worry James and spoil his beautiful sermons who,it is that deals with them. When there is money to give, he gives it : when we have to refuse to give money, I refuse it. I build a castle of comfort and luxury and love for him, and stand like a guard always to keep away little vulgar cares from him. I make him master here, though he does not know it, and could not tell you a moment ago how he became master here. (With sweet irony.) And when he thought 1 might go away with you, his only anxiety was—what should become of me. And to tempt me to stay he offered me (leaning forward to stroke his hair lovingly at each phrase. His strength for my defense, his industry for my livelihood, his dignity for my position his—(taking pity) ah, I am mixing up your beautiful rhythmical sentences and spoiling them, am I not, darling? (She lays her cheek lovingly against his)

Questions :

(i) Who is speaking and to whom?
(ii) What has spoiled Candida's boy since his birth?
(iii) Which pictures of James at school and college have been mentioned here?
(iv) How is Candida all in one for James?
(v) When does James give sermon?
(vi) What does James offer Candida to tempt to stay?

Find out a word from the passage which means :

(vii) situations
(viii) cut
(ix) worries

PASSAGE : 3

Studies serve for delight, for ornament, and ability. Their chief use for delight, is in privates and retiring; for ornament, is in discourse, and for ability, is in the judgement and disposition of business. For expert men can execute. and perhaps judge of particulars, one by one; but the general counsels, and the plots and marshalling of affairs, come best from those that are learned. To spend too much time in studies is sloth; to use them too much for ornament, is affectation; to make judgement wholly by their rules, is the humour of a scholar. They perfect nature, and are .perfected by experience : for natural abilities are like natural plants that need pruning by study; and studies themselves do give forth directions too much at large, except they be bounded in by expenence. Crafty men condemn studies, simple men admire them, and wise men use them; for they teach not their, own use; but that is a wisdom without them, and above them, won by observation. Read not to contradict and confute; nor to believe and take for granted; not to find talk and discourse; but to weigh and consider. Some books are to be tasted, others to be swallowed, and some few to be chewed and digested, that is, some books are to be read only in parts, others to be read, but not curiously; and some few to be read v'holly, and with diligence and attention. Some books also may be read by deputv and *extracts* made of them by others, but that would be only in the less important arguments. and the meaner sort of books, else distilled books are like common distilled waters, flashy things. Reading makes a full man; conference ready man; and writing an exact man. And therefore, if a man write little, he had need have a great memory; if he confer little, he had need have a present wit, and he read little, he had need have much cunning, to seem to know that he does not. Histories make man wise; poets witty; the mathematics subtle; natural philosophy deep; moral grave, logic and rhetoric able to contend. Abound studio in mores : [Studies pass into the character.] Nay there is no stand or impediment in the wit, but may be wrought out by fit studies : like as diseases of the body may have appropriate exercises. Bowling is good for the stone and reins, shooting for the lungs and breast; gentle walling for the stomach; riding for the head; and the like. So if a man's wit be wandering, let him study the mathematics; for in demonstrations, if his wit be called away never so little, he must begin again. If his wit be not apt to distinguish or find differences, let him study the schoolmen; for they are cymini sectores. If he be not apt to bear over matters, and to call up one thing to prove and illustrate another, let him study the lawyers' cases. So every defect of the mind may have a special receipt.

Questions :

(i) What do studies serve for?
(ii) What does the author say about crafty, simple and wise men?
(iii) How, according to the author, should we read?
(iv) What are the author's thoughts about books?
(v) What is the role of reading, conference and writing for a man?
(vi) How do different branches of knowledge contribute in man's 'making?

Find out a word from the passage which means :

(vii) most important
(viii) respect somebody for what they are or what they have done
(ix) something that delays or stops the progress of something

ENGLISH

PRACTICE SET

Answers to Passage : 1

(a) **NOTES :**

Positive Health

(A) DEFINITION
  (i) A person is fit physically and mentally, contented, and harmonious.

(B) STATUS IN DEVELOPED COUNTRIES
  (i) Poor despite better nutritional and environmental status because of discontented and disharmonious life.

(C) STATUS IN DEVELOPING COUNTRIES
  (i) Poor because of lower nutritional and environmental status.

(D) HOW TO ACHIEVE IT IN DEVELOPING COUNTRIES
  (i) Know body functions.
  (ii) Get better nutritional and environmental status
  (iii) Have proper education

(b) **SUMMARY :**

Title : Positive Health

A person who is fit physically and mentally, contented, and harmonious enjoys positive health. Its status in developed countries is poor despite better nutritional and environmental status because of discontented and disharmonious life. Its status in developing countries is also poor because bf lower nutritional and environmental status. Here it can be achieved by Mowing body functions, getting better nutritional and environmental status and having proper education.

Answers to Passage : 2

(a) **NOTES :**

Yoga, An Approach To Equilibrium

(A) SEVEN SCHOOLS OF YOGA
  (i) In 'Yoga Sutras' Patanjali expounded Raj Yoga, Hatha Yoga, Mantra Yoga, Bhakti Yoga etc.
  (ii) Yoga studies fluctuations of mind

(B) APPROACH TO EQUILIBRIUM
  (i) Through devotion to God
  (ii) Through modern techniques of Mental Hygiene
  (iii) For self-knowledge and internal mental balance

(b) **SUMMARY :**

Title : Yoga, An Approach to Equilibrium

Yoga is an approach to equilibrium. There are seven schools of yoga. Patanjali has expounded these in his book 'Yoga Sutras'. Raj Yoga, Hatha Yoga, Mantra Yoga, Bhakti Yoga schools commands much importance and others don't. According to Patanjali yoga studies the fluctuations of mind. Yoga as an approach achieves equilibrium through devotion to God and through modern techniques of Mental Hygiene. Yoga students strive for self-knowledge and internal mental balance.

Answers to Passage : 3

(a) **NOTES :**

Success

(A) BY CONCENTRATION, LABOUR, THROUGHESS, PATIENCE AND PERFECTION
  (i) Habits of application, study and methodical work.
  (ii) Precise manner.

FACTUAL PASSAGES

(B) BY SECURING EFFICIENCY
    (i) Careful arrangement and execution.

(C) BY A LONG TRAIL OF PASSIONATE EFFORTS
    (i) Be toilsome

(b) SUMMARY :

Title : Success

Success comes by concentration, labour, thoroughness, patience and perfection. Habits of application, study, methodical work and precise manner are helpful. Success is ensured by securing efficiency. Careful arrangement and execution helps in it. Success is also achieved by a long trail of passionate efforts. Tiresomeness assists in it.

Answers to Passage : 4

(a) NOTES :

Modern Life And Manners

(A) LIVING AND THINKING
    (i) Sophisticated, artificial, complex, deceitful
    (ii) Low thinking

(B) CHARACTER
    (i) Face—no index of mind.
    (ii) Expert psychologists can study.
    (iii) World full of cheats and robbers.
    (iv) Make belief and show business.

(C) NEW GENERATION
    (i) Clear and smart
    (ii) Beyond recognition

(D) MANNERS
    (i) Know good manners and possess.
    (ii) Maintain standards of dress and make up.
    (iii) No welcome and respect without proper manners.
    (iv) Good personality—clean dress and body, brushed hair, good conversation.

(E) VALUES LOST
    (i) Simplicity, innocence, honesty
    (ii) Intelligent to simpleton

(b) SUMMARY :

Title : Modern Life And Manners

Modern life is sophisticated, complex, artificial, deceitful and full of cheats and robbers. The character of a man can be studied only by expert psychologists from the outlook. The new generation is clear, smart and beyond recognition. Very few people depend on character and integrity. Good manners are important to possess. One have to maintain minimum standards of dress and make up without which there is no welcome anywhere. Tactful show of manners earn respect. Good personality includes clean dress and body, brushed hair, power of speech, patience of hearing others. It is important for success in life. Simplicity, innocence, honesty etc. have lost their values in modern society.

ENGLISH

Answers to Passage : 5

(a) **NOTES :**

The Art of Effective Listening

(A) **EFFECTIVE LISTENING**
  (i) Needs energy to concentrate on hearing
  (ii) Concentrate on understanding

(B) **FAILURE OF INCOMPETENT LISTENERS**
  (i) Their attention drifts
  (ii) Find counter arguments
  (iii) Compete, then filter
  (iv) Miss parts of message
  (v) Personal feelings override

(C) **KEYS TO EFFECTIVE LISTENING**
  (i) Art of concentrate's
  (ii) Need of determination
  (iii) Mental and physical alertness

(D) **INTENSIVE NOTE TAKING AN AID TO CONCENTRATION**
  (i) Capturing critical headings and sub-headings
  (ii) Note-taking helpful to speaker and listener
  (iii) Speaker can make effective use of pauses.

(E) **POSTURE OF THE LISTENER HELPS**
  (i) Upright posture helps listener's concentrate's
  (ii) Speaker too takes it to be a positive feature

(b) **SUMMARY :**

Title : The Art of Effective Listening

Effective speaking depends on effective listening. The latter depends on energy to hear and understand. Incompetent listeners' attention drifts. They find counter arguments, compete and then filter. They miss parts of the message which they find inconvenient to their own opinion. Over-riding personal feelings come in the way of understanding the message. Art of concentration is the first key. It needs determination. Mental and physical alertness help concentration. Posture is more important than mere fitness. Intensive note-taking helps both the listener and the speaker.

Answers to Passage : 6

(a) **NOTES :**

False Friends And True Friends

(A) **FALSE FRIEND**
  (i) Regards one's table but stands alone in need

(B) **TRUE FRIEND**
  (i) Shields against the adversary

FACTUAL PASSAGES

    (C) TAKE NOT COUNSEL FROM
        (i)   That counselled a way to suit himself
        (ii)   That wishes to watch thy misfortune
        (iii)   That has jealousy
        (iv)   A coward about war, merchant about exchange, buyer about selling, niggard about benevolence, unmerciful man about kindliness, sluggard about work.

    (D) TAKE COUNSEL FROM
        (i)   A Godly man
        (ii)   He who grieves when you stumble
        (iii)   Of thine own heart

(b) SUMMARY :

Title : False Friends And True Friends

Friends can be false or true. A false friend regards one's table but stands alone in need. A true friend always shields you against the adversary. In life you shouldn't take counsel from a man who counsels a way to suit himself, or who wishes to watch your misfortune or who has jealousy of you. Never take counsel from a coward about war, merchant about exchange, buyer about selling, niggard about benevolence, unmerciful man about kindness and sluggard about work. Always ke counsel from a Godly man or he who grieves when you stumble or your own heart.

Answers to Passage : 7

(a) NOTES :

Swami Vivekananda

    (A) BIRTH, PARENTAGE, TEMPERAMENT
        (i)   Born in an aristocratic Bengali Kayastha family of Calcutta on 12 Jan. 1863
        (ii)   Rational father, religious mother
        (iii)   Inclination towards spirituality

    (B) JOINED A GURU, UNDERTOOK TOUR
        (i)   Joined Guru Ramkrishna Paramhansa
        (ii)   Undertook tour of India

    (C) ATTENDED CHICAGO'S PARLIAMENT OF RELIGIONS 1893
        (i)   Instant celebrity in America
        (ii)   Spread Vedanta Philosophy in US, UK for three years

    (D) DEATH
        (i)   4 July 1902

(b) SUMMARY :

Title : Swami Vivekananda

Swami Vivekananda was born in an aristocratic Bengali Kayastha family of Calcutta on 12 Jan. 1863. He had rational father and religious mother. He had inclination towards spirituality. He joined Guru Ramkrishna Paramhansa. He taught him non-dualism and God realization. After the death of his Guru he undertook the tour of India. He got first hand experience. In 1893 he attended Chicago's Parliament of Religions. He became an instant celebrity in Ameri For three years he spread Vedanta Philosophy in US and UK. He died on 4 July 1902.

Unit-4

RE-ARRANGING TUMBLED UP PARTS OF A SENTENCE

RE-ARRANGING TUMBLED UP PARTS OF A SENTENCE

Rearrange these parts which are lablled P,Q and S to produce a grammatically correct and coherent sentence.

1. It is better _____.
   P. to keep the refrigerator
   Q. In a well ventilated space
   R. and
   S. not
   T. in a closed cavity
   (a) SPQRT   (b) PQRST
   (c) PTRSQ   (d) QRTSP

2. Moisture and humidity _____.
   P. controls
   Q. retain
   R. the freshness of fruits and vegetables
   S. in a refrigerator help
   (a) QSPR   (b) PSQR
   (c) SQPR   (d) SRPQ

3. It you require assistance _____.
   P. promptly and politely
   Q. ask for customer service associates
   R. to help our customers
   S. who have instructions.
   (a) SQPR   (b) QPSR
   (c) QSRP   (d) SQRP

4. People _____.
   P. at his clinic   Q. went to him
   R. of all status
   S. for medicine and treatment
   (a) QPRS   (b) RPQS
   (c) RQSP   (d) QRPS

5. little _____.
   P. that she had been
   Q. stood by in all tough times
   R. did she realise
   S. by a friend whom she had
   (a) RPSQ   (b) RSQP
   (c) QSRP   (d) QSPR

6. The majestic sandalwood bed _____.
   P. belongs to a royal family
   Q. which is very well maintained
   R. that is now impoverished
   S. but not without some pricle
   (a) RSPQ   (b) SPRQ
   (c) SQRP   (d) QPRS

7. Towards early morning_____.
   P. So that the sky was lighted with
   Q. and the clouds drifted away
   R. the rain stopped
   S. incredible moonlight
   (a) SQRP   (b) SQPR
   (c) RQPS   (d) SPQR

8. The parents_____.
   P. When they were in france
   Q. to their three children
   R. for seven years
   S. should not teach hindi
   (a) SRPQ (b) PRSQ (c) SQPR (d) PQRS

9. I can_____.
   P. hear the spokes person all right
   Q. I could see her
   R. But I wish
   S. as she lashes out at the opposition party
   (a) PRSQ (b) PQRS (c) PQSR (d) PRQS

10. The effectiveness of a show _____.
    P. The needs of the audience
    Q. is judged by
    R. and by its relation to
    S. its theme
    (a) PSQR (b) QRPS (c) PQRS (d) QSRP

ANSWER
1. b   2. b   3. c
4. c   5. a   6. d
7. c   8. c   9. d
10. d

RE-ARRANGING

REARRANGE TUMBLED SENTENCES SOLVED, EXERCISES -:

Q.1 Arrange the words in the correct order to form meaningful sentences.

1. dog/Rahul/with his / Pet / Playing / enjoys.
2. to / the company / goods / vitnam / exparts.
3. every/dilicious/father cooks/evening / pasta.
4. Brother / an / wants / be / my / astronaut / to .
5. Everything / will / sense/ make / perfect / someday.
6. Ship / violently / the storm / rocked / the.
7. Masterpiece / artist / painstakingly / the / his / warked at
8. gift / fru / a / dad/ offerd / firm / by the / was.
9. I read / paper / in the / burglar / beer/ caught / had/ the / that.
10. nightfall / began / cricketers/ the / at / their pircing calls.
11. work / ahat / he / of coconat / made / fiber / his / on / hard.
12. parts / many / coffa/ popular in / world / the / is / very/ of.
13. cave / could/ explare/ not / they / tarch / the / without / a .
14. the / storn / shid / damaged / the / was / during.
15. the dog / tames / talking / sat next to / himself to.

Answer :

1. Rahul enjoys playing with his pet dog.
2. The company exports goods to vitnam.
3. Father cooks dilious pasta every evening.
4. My brother wants to be an astronaut.
5. Someday everything will make perfect sense.
6. The starm rocked the ship violently.
7. The artist painstakingly worked at his masterpiece.
8. Dad was offered a fur gift by the film.
9. I read in the paper that the burglar had been caught.
10. The cricketers began their piercing calls at nightfall.
11. He wore a hat made of coconat fiber on his head
12. Coffee is very popular in many parts of the world.
13. They could not explore the cave without a torch.
14. The shed was damaged during the storm.
15. Tames sat next to the dog talking to himself.

ENGLISH

PRACTICE PAPER-01

(READING)
READ THE PASSAGE

1. If one early June moring you are suddenly stopped in your walk by a ringing pip-piu-pie-pee piu piu call coming from the trees in your heart suddenly lifted. Look around and you may see two large, handsome, black-and-white birds with long coattails chasing each other among the trees. They are pied cuckoos, that have come from Africa and are said to announce the arrival of the greatest show on earth the indian moonsoon. Be assured the curtains will rise in month or so.

2. To get a proper view of the onset of the monsoon you really need to be stationed on the costline of india or up in the hills. The grand show of great clouds approaches like an airborne army, preceded by cool breeze ,filling the air with electric charge so that you will very happy. spare of lighting flicker in the sky in the sound of thunder makes you feel exited. And than, it pours. The cracked earth without any green cover sucks down the flood of water-and than mother nature goes mad. Seeds scattered of buried like grains of sand of pebbles in the ground suddenly comes to life .Shoots of plants skywards ,roots plunge into the soft, spounge earth sucking up water and nutrience its a hint the grasshoppers have been waiting for. And bugs ,beetles, caterpillars, centipedes, etc. emerge in their billions, feasting on the fresh green in the fields(to the annoyance of many a farmers)as also on each other.

3. There are miracles and there is music too: singing golden fogs apperaring in large numbers in rain filled ditch, talking part in group song that bollywood would have envied. They vanish the very next day. They'd been waiting patiently all through the blistering summer, deep underground, conserving whatever moisture they had soaked up. Fireflies wink through the trees in the hills, sending their greenish signals to one another in codes as precise as any we may use for our most secret messages.

4. All this is what the birds have been waiting for. Most birds have spent the spring and summer courting and now it's time to settle down. Baby birds need a lot of high protien at frequent intervals, which the rich supply of insect life of happily provides: Caterpillars are eaten up in millions, as are furry moths, eathworms slurped down like noodles, spiky dragonflies beaten to bits to soften them up into baby food. The long-legged storks and herons - get busy with fishing. As for the bugs like lions are tigers in the jungles: thet too had it relatively easy during the summer when their thirsty prey came to the water-holes. Now, with water eaisly availabe, in streams and ponds all over, they need to work harder for their meals. But yes, this is, perhaps, compensated by the arrival of baby deer - and fawns are sweet and soft, not very experienced in the merciless ways of rhw lions and tigers , even if they may seem more like a snack than a main course meal. The animals get a rest from us, parks and sanctuaries too close down, not so much out because the roads become impassable.

5. And than, just as you are beginning to get tired of green mould on your shoes, belts and bags and all of the sniffles and snuffles that the rains also brings (bacteria and viruses also love this season)the clouds began to disperse and float awys in large armies. But before this happens, atleast ones, do go out in the midst of a downpore, race your face to the heavens and dance and sing and celebrate this, the greatest show on earth.

PRACTICE PAPERS

1.1 answer each of the questions given below by choosing the most appropriate option: (1x5=5)
   (a) The winged messengers from Africa:
      (i) bring rain from Africa
      (ii) brings the message that the rains are comingsoon.
      (iii) create alot of horrible noise.
      (iv) are not welcome.
   (b) Baby birds benefit from the rains because:
      (i) the mummy bird cannot fly in the rain.
      (ii) they need a lot of noodles.
      (iii) the rain brings alot of insects which they eat.
      (iv) They like wet nests
   (c) Humans dont visit the animals in sanctuaries during the rainy season because:
      (i) humans dont like to get wet.
      (ii) the paths to the sanctuaries become waterlogged.
      (iii) baby animals are born in the sanctuaries.
      (iv) humans get bitten during the rainy season.
   (d) The green mould that grows onleather comes:
      (i) from the creepy insects that come with the rain.
      (ii) beacause grass becomes very green during the rainy season .
      (iii) because of the moisture in the air during the rainy season.
      (iv) from fluffy clouds in the sky.
   (e) Lions and tigers have easy life during summer beacause
      (i) there is easy availability of water everywhere
      (ii) they are not able to catch fawns
      (iii) humans visit the sanctuaries a lot during summer
      (iv) thirsty animals come to the waterholes as easy preys.

1.2 Fill in the blanks: (1x4=4)
   (1) pied------------have come from Africa
   (2) the greatest show on the earth is the Indian-------.
   (3) .... wink through the trees in the hills.
   (4) The storks and----------get busy with the fishing.

1.3 Pick out the words/phrases from the passage which are similar in meaning to the following: (1x3=3)
   (i) declare (para1)
   (ii) disappear(para3)
   (iii) a heavy fall of rain(para5)

Direction for question 16 to 20 correct the following sentences

16. He has joined a six months course.
17. of gaya and patna which town is hotter?
18. A lokshabha passed a bill today.
19. The tourist city has many placeses worth seeing
20. Beauty of virdawan garden at the night is worth seeing.

Direction for questions 21 to 25 choose the alternative which best expresses the meaning of given idiom/phrases.

21. to get into hot waters
   (a) to suffer a financial loss
   (b) to be inpatient
   (c) to get into trouble
   (d) to be confused stage of mind
22. The green eyed monster :
   (a) the creature of the sea
   (b) animals with a green eyes
   (c) personal jealousy
   (d) to get into trouble
23. to keep once temper:
   (a) to be in good mood
   (b) to become angry
   (c) to preserve once energy
   (d) none of these

ENGLISH

24. A wet blanket:
    (a) a man who is always drunk
    (b) a wife who is cold to her husband
    (c) to wear black and white clothes
    (d) none of these

25. To lose once bearings:
    (a) to lose once strengnth
    (b) to become sick and tried
    (c) to be uncertain of once position
    (d) to become hopeless

    Directions for questions 26 to 30 choose the word that can be substituted for the given groups of words.

26. One who belives in fate
    (a) Fatalist   (b) alphabet
    (c) reveille   (d) stroll

27. A cheif character ina story or drama
    (a) anthology   (b) whole some
    (c) propagonist   (d) precaution

28. Winding sheet of a corpse
    (a) customary   (b) shroud
    (c) excursion   (d) malnutrition

29. One who abandons his religios faith
    (a) apostate   (b) prostate
    (c) profane   (d) agnostic

30. A hater of knowledge and learning
    (a) Bibliophile   (b) philologist
    (c) misogynist   (d) misologist

    Directions for questions 31 to 35 rearrange the given sentence in correct order

31. (p) moisture and humidity
    (Q) controls, refain
    (R) the freshness of fruits and vegetables
    (S) in a refrigeratear help.
    (a) QSPR   (b) PSQR
    (c) SQPR   (d) SRPQ

32. (p) A little suffering never hurt anyone
    (Q) and already she was begning to
    (R) have a new appreciation for the comforts
    (S) that she had once taken for granted]
    (a) PQRS   (b) RQPS
    (c) SQRP   (d) QPSR

33. (P) in the middle square sits the chair man
    (Q) of the committee, the most important
    (R) of onse side of the
    (s) person in the room
    (a) PSQR   (b) RPQS
    (c) SRQP   (d) SPQR

34. people......
    (P) at his clinic
    (Q) went to him
    (R) of all status
    (S) for medicine and treatmeant
    (a) QPRS   (b) RPQS
    (c) RQSP   (d) QRPS

35. (p) The majestic sandal wood bed belongs to royal family
    (q) which is very well maintain
    (R) that is know improverished
    (s) but not without some pride
    (A) RSPQ   (B) SPRQ
    (C) SQRP   (D) QPRS

    Directions for questions 36 to 39 similar in meaning

36. Barbarian
    (a) desire   (b) anxiety
    (c) illitrate   (d) cruel

37. calamity
    (a) tragedy   (b) relaxed
    (c) duplicate   (d) polite

38. Apathetic
    (a) emotionless   (b) demon
    (c) dismount   (d) decrease

39. Zest
    (a) Appetite   (b) diagnose
    (c) comfortable   (d) fragile

    Direction for question 40 to 45 select the word or phrase from the given choices that is most nearly opposite to word given in the question

40. ruthless
    (a) mindful   (b) compassionate
    (c) majestic   (d) merciless

41. rectify
    (a) adjust (b) amend
    (c) falsify (d) improve

42. Eternity
    (a) perpetuity (b) yonder
    (c) aeon (d) epheneral

43. compulsary
    (a) ugly (b) top
    (c) changeable (d) voluntary

44. ancestor
    (a) descentant (b) amuse
    (c) exciting (d) death

45. Abundance
    (a) departure (b) intentional
    (c) lack
    (d) elementary

Direction for questions 46 to 50 read each sentence to find out any grammatical error in it, if the answer is no error

46. what a better way(a)/of taking care than(b)/ensure good health(c)/good health

47. passes through a fores (a)/to famous monument(b)/the road (c)/no error(d)

48. if you had read(a)/the relevent literature carefully, (b)/you would have answer(c)/most of the question correctly(d)/no error(e)

49. suresh babu who is living(a)/in this town since1955(b)/is a well known scholar of history(c)/and a disticguise musician(d)/no error

50. the neighbour along with his children(a)/is going tonight(b)/to see a tajmahal(c)/at agara(d)/no error(e).

PRACTICE PAPER-02

Direction for question 1 to 4 : rearrange the given sentence in the correct order

1. A: A day to celebrate all father's
   B: What began as one women's
   C: Tribute to her dad turned
   D: Into a life-long mission for
   (a) ADBC (b) BCDA
   (c) BDCA (d) ABCD

2. P: Towards early morning the rain stopped
   Q: And the clouds drifted away
   R: So that the sky war lighted with
   S: Incredible moonlight
   (a) SRQP (b) SQPR
   (c) PQRS (d) SPQR

3. I can ......
   P: Hear the spokes person all right
   Q: I could see her
   R: But I wish
   S: AS she lashes cut at the opposition party
   (a) PRSQ (b) PQRS
   (c) QPSR (d) PQRS

4. The effectiveness of a show.....
   P: The needs of the audience
   Q: Is judged by
   R: And by its relation to
   S: Its theme
   (a) PSQR (b) QRPS
   (c) PQRS (d) QSRP

Directions for question 5 to 8 : in each following sentences, an expression is given underline which may be or not be grammatically correct . choose the option which can correct the given sentence. If no change is required mark "No improvement"

5. They feel very proudly that their son had won the match
   (a) Feel very proud   (c) Feel pride
   (b) Felt very proud   (d) No improvement

6. Ajay is the _____ boy in the class
   (a) Clever   (c) Cleverest
   (b) Cleverer (d) Cleverless

7. Today is the _____ night of the week
   (a) cold   (c) colder
   (b) coldest (d) colds

8. She is becoming _____ 8 more beautiful
   (a) much (c) more
   (b) must (d) mostfull

Direction for question 9 to 13 : choose the alternatine which best expresses the meaning of the given Idoim/ phrase

9. To make clean breast of
   (a) to gain prominence
   (b) To praise oneself
   (c) To confess without of reserve
   (d) To destroy before it blooms
   (e) None of these

10. To keeps one's temper
    (a) To becomes hungry
    (b) To be in good mood
    (c) To preserve ones energy
    (d) To be aloof from
    (e) None of these

11. To catch a tartar
    (a) To trap wanted criminal with great difficulty
    (b) To catch a dangerous person
    (c) To meet with disoster
    (d) To deal with a person who is more than one's match
    (e) None of these

12. To drive home
    (a) To find one's roots
    (b) To return to place of rest
    (c) Back to original position
    (d) To emphasise
    (e) None of these

13. To have an axe to grind
    (a) A private end to serve
    (b) To fail to arouse interest
    (c) To have no result
    (d) To work for both sides
    (e) None of these

Direction of question 14 to 18 : choose the **incorr**ectly spelt word from the given options

14. (a) Inventor (c) Defense
    (b) Usable (d) Annual
15. (a) Potassium (c) Parasology
    (b) Possibility (d) Preamble
16. (a) Pursue (c) Persuade
    (c) persuit (d) peruse
17. (a) Sanguinery (c) temporary
    (b) Itinerary (d) necessary
18. (a) Deceive (c) conceive
    (b) perceive (d) receive

Direction for question 19 to 23: choose the correctly word that is most nearly opposite to the words given in the question

19. The antomy of 'approve' is -
    (a) destory (c) generate
    (b) cancel (d) None of above
20. The antonym of 'buy' is -
    (a) sell (c) bring (b) gain (d) profit
21. The antonym of 'quiet' is-
    (a) strong (c) excited
    (b) calm (d) None of the above
22. The anatonym of 'neglect' is -
    (a) Attention (c) refuse
    (b) ignore (d) None of above
23. The anatonym of 'clever' is-
    (a) angry (c) cunning
    (b) naughty (d) stupid
24. Choose the most appropriate set of verbs for the blank below
    Don't make a noise; the child _____ now (sleep) . It _____ in july . it _____ now (rain). Our publisher generally _____Hindi but today he _____ English (speak).
    My wife and I _____to the cinema every saturday. (go)
    (a) sleep, sleeping (b) rain, raining
    (c) speak,speaking (d) go,going
25. Choose the underline clause; whichever place you like you can go
    (a) Noun clause (c) Adverb clause
    (b) Relative clause (d) Verbless clause
26. Select the most suitable synonym for the words panorama
    (a) View (c) feeling
    (b) eminent (d) circle

PRACTICE PAPER-03

Direction for question 1 to 10:
Select the most appropriate option to fill in the blanks

1. Only the blood stained road was a witness _____his assassination
   (a) of   (b) to   (c) at   (d) on

2. I continued to smile_____his threats
   (a) at   (b) on   (c) upon   (d) over

3. There was a ____sight in Jamshedpur.(lovely)
   (a) love   (b) loved
   (c) loviliness   (d) lovely

4. Milk is_____to tea (preferable)
   (a) preferableless   (b) prefer
   (c) preferable   (d) preferful

5. The work men _____ the road near our house. (repair)
   (a) is reaparing   (b) are repairing
   (c) was repairing   (d) has repairing

6. MY brother_____ tomorrow (arrive)
   (a) is arriving   (b) has arrived
   (c) was aeeiving   (d) had arrived

7. Our favourite_____won the match
   (a) Game   (b) Tearcher
   (c) Team   (d) Coach

8. A____of robbers entered the city at night
   (a) criminal   (b) gang
   (c) gangester   (d) Mafia

9. The_____was a fine one
   (a) Crew   (b) Group   (c) Army   (d) A man

10. The_____was defeated
    (a) Platoon   (b) Company
    (c) Civil   (d) Army

Choose the correct words to complete the sentence.

11. I know_____well what I'm going to do when I reach the lab next week
    (a) totally   (b) absolute
    (c) very   (d) less

12. Anatonym of 'Acquite'
    (a) unacquite   (b) convict
    (c) Disadvantages   (d) retain

13. Choose the correct spelling
    (a) vertual   (b) virtual
    (c) vertuall   (d) vurtuall

14. Synonym of 'orator' ?
    (a) speaker   (b) Master
    (c) Examiner   (d) Interviewer

15. which is the nearest meaning of phrase in respect of ?
    (a) in despite of   (b) in a few words
    (c) popular   (d) in the eye of

16. I am just' a small fire' in the office
    (a) Peon
    (b) small creature
    (c) person of little importance
    (d) Joker

17. Identify the verb type
    They made me call the police
    (a) present participle   (b) past participle
    (c) Infinite   (d) perfect participle

18. correct the following sentence. Both Aditiya as well as Aditi came
    (a) And   (b) but   (c) while   (d) that

19. pick out the conjuction. I like her beause she is beautiful
    (a) but   (b) like   (c) because   (d) is

20. Find out the error ?
    (a) Had I realised
    (b) That is was such a long way
    (c) I would take a taxy
    (d) No error

INFORMAL vs FORMAL WORDS

INFORMAL	FROMAL
Ask	Enquire
Ask for	Request
Book	Reserve
Check	Verify
Get	Receive
Help	Assist
Need	Request
Deal with	Handle
Tell	inform
Wall for	Awoll
Fight	Combat
Use	Consume
Go	Deport
Say sorry	Apologise
Start	Commence
End	Terminote
Try	Endeovour

INFORMAL	FROMAL
Tough	Difficult
Exploin	Elucidote
Set out	Display
Throw out	Eject
Old	Elderly
Say	Express
Afraid	Fearful
In the end	Finally
But	However
Wrong	Incorrect
Go up	Increase
At first	Initially
Mad	Insane
Lucky	Fortunate
Smart	Inteligent
Small	Diminetive
Cheap	inexpensive

INFORMAL	FROMAL
Right	Correct
A bit	A little
Away	Absent
Let	Allow
Seem	Appear
Climb	Ascend
Boat up	Assault
Eager	Avid
Call off	Cancel
Stop	Ceose
Big/Large	Enormous
Help	Aid/ Assist
Friendly	Amlable
Expect	Anticipate
Fall out	Quarrel
Speed up	Accelerate
Okay/Ok	Acceptable

INFORMAL	FROMAL
Sick	ill
Ast out	Invite
Go away	Leave
Free	Liberate
Deal with	Manage
Bad	Nogative
See	Porcrive
Happy	Pleased
Give up	Quit
Older	Senior
Use	Utilize
Empty	Vacant
Enough	Sufficient
End	Terminate
At once	Immediately
Look Into	Investigate
Chance	Opportunity

INFORMAL	FROMAL
Dore	Challenge
Kids	Chidren
Settle for	Choose
Round	Circular
Pick up	Collect
Think of	Conceive
Link up	Connect
Think about	Consider
Build	Construct
Refer to	Consult
Hurt	Damage
Go down	Decrease
Set down	Deposit
Want	Desire
Lack	Deficiency
Show	Demonstrate
Brave	Gaurogeou

www.ingramcontent.com/pod-product-compliance
Lightning Source LLC
LaVergne TN
LVHW070531070526
838199LV00075B/6754